The Garden Cart

Compiled and Edited by
Judith Bosley

Cover by
Steven Miles

Illustrations by
Christine Moore Currie

LEB Inc.
Boise, Idaho

Copyright © 1994 Judith Ann Bosley
All rights reserved
First Printing June 1994
Printed in the United States of America
ISBN: 0-930809-17-3

LEB Inc.

Boise, Idaho 83706

Your garden cart runneth over with the fruits of your harvest. Now flip through the pages of our Garden Cart for both old and new ideas about how to fix those treasures. The alphabetical listing will help you find recipes for today's harvest. From early spring and *Asparagus Soup*, to fall and *Frosted Zucchini Bars*, enjoy every bite of the most perfectly ripe and delicious garden vegetables; those you grow yourself.

J. Bosley

STIR-FRYING VEGETABLES

To stir-fry vegetables, heat 1-2 tablespoons of cooking oil (olive or peanut are best) in a heavy skillet or wok and add vegetables. Stir over high heat, stirring or "flipping" almost constantly until crisp tender.

STEAMING VEGETABLES

Steaming is more satisfactory for white, yellow and red vegetables than for green ones which may turn olive-green or brown. Steamed vegetables are prepared by placing them on a rack over boiling water and cooking with a tight cover. Cooking time may be a little longer than for boiling.

BROILING VEGETABLES

Broiling is a quick, easy method to use for raw sliced vegetables such as potatoes, onions, eggplant and tomatoes. Preheat broiler and place vegetables on greased broiler rack. Brush with butter or oil. Place rack 3 inches below the source of heat and broil until vegetables are tender, turning once and salting.

PREVENTING STRONG FLAVORS

Vegetables such as cabbage, broccoli, cauliflower, Brussels sprouts and turnips have strong flavors and strong odors, and can develop bad flavors if overcooked. Therefore, cook these vegetables uncovered to allow substances responsible for this to go off in the steam. Remember, however, to add additional water to compensate for the steam and to prevent burning.

MICROWAVE TIPS

* Salt toughens vegetables in the microwave, so add salt after cooking.
* Always pierce vegetables with skins before cooking to prevent them from exploding.
* Arrange vegetables in a circle for more even cooking.
* Cover vegetables with a glass lid or pierced plastic wrap for quicker and more even cooking.
* Do not overcook vegetables. Vegetables continue to cook after they are removed from the oven, so make allowances in cooking time if serving will be delayed.

CONTENTS

Asparagus Soup..1
Asparagus with Wine Sauce..2
Cheesy Asparagus Casserole...3
Oriental Asparagus Salad...4
Jean's Asparagus Salad...5
Bean-Mushroom Medley...6
Green Bean Casserole...7
Green Bean In Swiss Cheese Sauce..8
Perky Lima Beans..9
Creole Lima Beans..10
Lima Luncheon..11
Beets and Pineapple..12
Beets in Sour Cream...13
Garden Borscht..14
Orange Glazed Beets..15
Pickled Beets...16
Broccoli Potato Soup...17
Marinated Broccoli Salad...18
Gardener's Special..19
Broccoli with Mustard Sauce...20
Broccoli and Rice Casserole..21
Cream Cheese and Broccoli..22
Broccoli with Herb Stuffing...23
Broccoli and Cauliflower Bake..24
Microwave Hollandaise for Sprouts...25
Brussels Sprouts with Lemon..26
Ever Ready Cold Slaw..27
Just Great Cabbage Salad..28
Crunchy Cabbage Salad...29
Mixed Up Crunchy Cabbage Salad...30
Cabbage Stir Fry...31
Fried Cabbage with Sour Cream..32
Sweet & Sour Cabbage...33
Fried Cabbage with Apple...34
Sweet and Sour Carrots...35
Carrots with Orange...36
Kitty's Carrot Salad..37

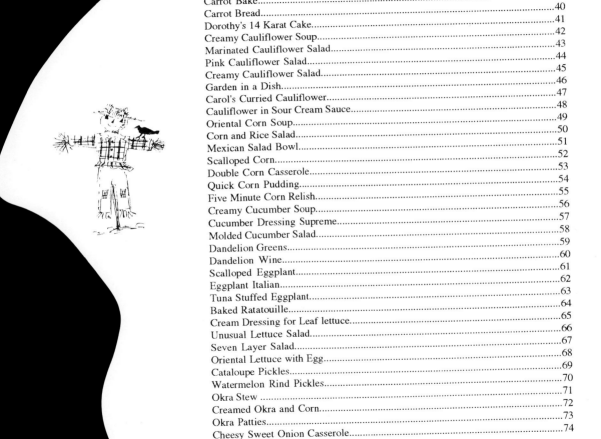

Carrot and Horseradish Casserole	38
Carrot Bake	39
Carrot Bread	40
Dorothy's 14 Karat Cake	41
Creamy Cauliflower Soup	42
Marinated Cauliflower Salad	43
Pink Cauliflower Salad	44
Creamy Cauliflower Salad	45
Garden in a Dish	46
Carol's Curried Cauliflower	47
Cauliflower in Sour Cream Sauce	48
Oriental Corn Soup	49
Corn and Rice Salad	50
Mexican Salad Bowl	51
Scalloped Corn	52
Double Corn Casserole	53
Quick Corn Pudding	54
Five Minute Corn Relish	55
Creamy Cucumber Soup	56
Cucumber Dressing Supreme	57
Molded Cucumber Salad	58
Dandelion Greens	59
Dandelion Wine	60
Scalloped Eggplant	61
Eggplant Italian	62
Tuna Stuffed Eggplant	63
Baked Ratatouille	64
Cream Dressing for Leaf lettuce	65
Unusual Lettuce Salad	66
Seven Layer Salad	67
Oriental Lettuce with Egg	68
Cataloupe Pickles	69
Watermelon Rind Pickles	70
Okra Stew	71
Creamed Okra and Corn	72
Okra Patties	73
Cheesy Sweet Onion Casserole	74

Dutch Onion Ring Salad	75
Deluxe Onion Pie	76
Parsley and Rice	77
Tabbouleh	78
Parship Casserole with Rosemary	79
Fresh Peas at their Best	80
Peas and Peanuts	81
Sweet-Pea Risotto	82
Green Pea Casserole	83
Creamed Peas and Potatoes	84
Sweet Red Pepper Soup	85
Hot Slaw Stuffed Peppers	86
Dilled Red Potato Salad	87
Sour Cream Potato Salad	88
Potato Cowder with Dumplings	89
Twice-Baked Potatoes	90
Mashed Potato Casserole	91
Potato and Carrot Skillet	92
Potatoes and Corn with Buttermilk	93
Parmesan Potatoes	94
Potatoes and Apples for Two	95
Potato Chocolate Cake	96
Pumpkin Bread	97
Pumpkin Squares	98
Fresh Pumpkin Pie with Pecans	99
Pumpkin Roll	100
Rhubarb Salad	101
Rhubarb Bread	102
Rubarb Up-Side-Down Cake	103
Rhubarb Pudding Cake	104
Rhubarb Crunch	105
Rhubarb Custard Meringue Pie	106
Rhubarb Orange Custard Pie	107
Rhubarb-Apple Pies	108
Strawberry Rhubarb Pie	109
Rutabaga Casserole	110
Mashed Rutabaga	111

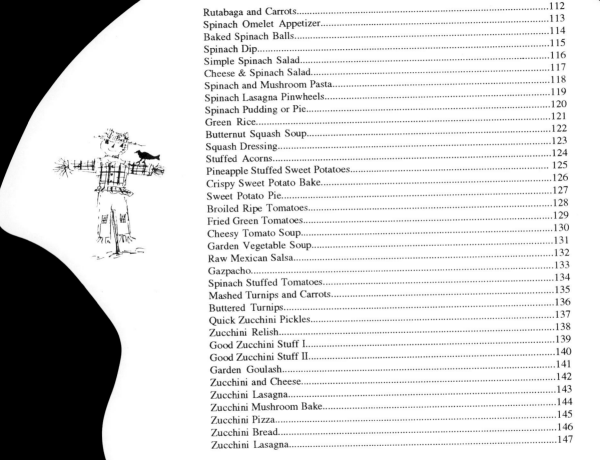

Rutabaga and Carrots	112
Spinach Omelet Appetizer	113
Baked Spinach Balls	114
Spinach Dip	115
Simple Spinach Salad	116
Cheese & Spinach Salad	117
Spinach and Mushroom Pasta	118
Spinach Lasagna Pinwheels	119
Spinach Pudding or Pie	120
Green Rice	121
Butternut Squash Soup	122
Squash Dressing	123
Stuffed Acorns	124
Pineapple Stuffed Sweet Potatoes	125
Crispy Sweet Potato Bake	126
Sweet Potato Pie	127
Broiled Ripe Tomatoes	128
Fried Green Tomatoes	129
Cheesy Tomato Soup	130
Garden Vegetable Soup	131
Raw Mexican Salsa	132
Gazpacho	133
Spinach Stuffed Tomatoes	134
Mashed Turnips and Carrots	135
Buttered Turnips	136
Quick Zucchini Pickles	137
Zucchini Relish	138
Good Zucchini Stuff I	139
Good Zucchini Stuff II	140
Garden Goulash	141
Zucchini and Cheese	142
Zucchini Lasagna	143
Zucchini Mushroom Bake	144
Zucchini Pizza	145
Zucchini Bread	146
Zucchini Lasagna	147

is for Asparagus

What's not to like about asparagus? Its low calorie, has vitamin C, is picture pretty and available almost all year in the markets. Look for smooth, round, tender green spears with closed tips. To prepare fresh asparagus, wash, then break off tough ends as far down as stalks snap easily. The tips cook more quickly than the stalks so there are various methods for cooking to get stalks tender without turning tips to mush.

Cook whole spears : Heat 1 inch salted water to boiling in deep narrow pan or coffeepot. Place asparagus bundle upright in pan. Heat to boiling; cook uncovered 5 minutes. Cover and cook until stalk ends are crisp-tender, 7-10 minutes more; drain.

Pieces: Cook lower stalk pieces uncovered in steamer or in 1 inch boiling salted water for 6 minutes. Add tips. Cover and cook until crisp-tender, 5-8 minutes longer; drain.

To microwave: Cover and microwave asparagus (spears and tips) and 1/4 cup water for 4 minutes; turn asparagus over. Cover and microwave until crisp-tender, 4-6 minutes more. Let stand 1 minute; drain. **Seasonings good with asparagus are lemon, sesame seed and tarragon.**

1 ASPARAGUS SOUP

A spring treat that you will make over and over again

1 lb fresh asparagus (about 1 C tips and 2 cups stalk pieces)
2 C water
3 C vegetable stock
1 medium onion, diced
4 T butter
4 T flour
2 C milk
salt and pepper

Cut tips off asparagus and microwave for three minutes or steam until tender crisp; set aside. Cut rest of asparagus stalks in pieces and cook in 2 cups water with onion until vegetables are tender. Purée undrained asparagus and onion mixture in blender. In sauce pan melt butter and add flour, stirring until smooth; stir in stock, asparagus mixture and milk. Heat until slightly thickened. Add asparagus tips and serve.
6-8 Servings.

2 ASPARAGUS WITH WINE SAUCE

Delicious sauce for a delicious vegetable

1 1/2 lb fresh asparagus
1/4 C dry white wine
1 T instant minced onion
3/4 C mayonnaise or salad dressing
1 T lemon juice
2 hard-cooked eggs, chopped

Cook either whole stalks or pieces as directed. Pour wine over onion in saucepan; stir in mayonnaise and lemon juice; heat just to boiling. Stir in eggs gently. Serve hot over asparagus. Serves 4-6.

3 CHEESY ASPARAGUS CASSEROLE

1 1/2 lbs fresh asparagus
3 T margarine
3 T flour
1 1/2 C milk
3 ozs cream cheese
4 ozs shredded Cheddar cheese
salt and pepper to taste
cracker or potato chip crumbs

Cut asparagus into 1 inch pieces and cook for 4 minutes; drain and place in a buttered baking dish. Melt margarine and blend in flour; gradually add milk and cook until thickened. Add cheeses and stir until melted. Season to taste and pour cheese sauce over asparagus. Top with crumbs and bake at 350° for 30 minutes. Serves 6.

4 ORIENTAL ASPARAGUS SALAD

2 lbs fresh asparagus
1/4 C soy sauce
1 t sugar

1 t vinegar
1/2 t salt
2 t sesame oil

Wash asparagus and discard tough ends of spears. Cut diagonally in 1 1/2 inch pieces and cook for 1 minute in boiling water; drain and plunge into cold water. Combine remaining ingredients in a large bowl, add asparagus and toss to coat well. Chill and toss again before serving.

5 JEAN'S ASPARAGUS SALAD MOLD

Unusual and delicious

6 stalk fresh asparagus
1 can asparagus soup
1, 8 oz pkg cream cheese
1, 3 oz pkg lime gelatin
1/2 C mayonnaise

1 t grated onion
3/4 C chopped celery
1/2 C chopped green pepper
1/2 C chopped nuts
1/4 C cold water

Slice asparagus thinly and cook just until tender-crisp; drain and cool. Heat soup; stir in gelatin, cheese and mayonnaise until smooth. Add remaining ingredients, pour mixture into prepared mold and chill. Serves 8-10.

is for Beans

See those little plants just hanging heavy with green or yellow snap beans? Next see them on your plate in many delicious forms. *Seasonings for snap beans are basil, dill, mint and oregano.*

6   BEAN-MUSHROOM MEDLEY

8 ozs fresh green beans
2 fresh medium carrots, cut into strips
1 medium onion, sliced
8 ozs fresh mushrooms, sliced

1/4 C margarine
1 t salt
1/2 t MSG (optional)
1/4 t garlic salt
1/8 t white pepper

Heat 1 inch water to boiling in 2-quart saucepan; add beans and carrots. Cover and simmer, until almost tender, about 12 minutes; drain.* Cook and stir onion and mushrooms in margarine over medium heat until almost tender; stir in beans, carrots, salt, monosodium glutamate, garlic salt and pepper. Cover and cook for 5 minutes. Serves 5-6.

7 GREEN BEAN CASSEROLE

Everyone's favorite

3 C green beans
1 can cream of mushroom soup
1/2 C milk
1-2 T soy sauce
1, 3 1/2 oz can French fried onions

In a casserole dish combine soup, milk and soy sauce. Stir in beans and 1/2 can onions. Bake at 350° for 25 minutes; stir. Top with remaining onions; bake 5 minutes more. Serves 6.

8 GREEN BEANS IN SWISS CHEESE SAUCE

1 1/2 lbs fresh green beans
1/4 C butter
1/4 C chopped onion
1/2 lb mushrooms, sliced
3 T flour
1/8 t each thyme and marjoram
salt and pepper to taste
1 C milk
1 C shredded Swiss cheese
1/2 C sherry

Steam beans until tender. Sauté onion and mushrooms in butter; add flour, seasonings and milk; cook until thickened. Stir in half of cheese. Remove from heat and add beans. Pour into a shallow casserole and sprinkle with rest of cheese. Bake uncovered at 400° for 25-30 minutes. Serves 6.

LIMA BEANS

TO PREPARE fresh limas: Wash and shell lima beans just before cooking. To shell beans, remove thin outer edge of pod with sharp knife or scissors. Beans will slip out.

TO COOK: Heat 1 inch salted water to boiling. Add beans. Heat to boiling and cook uncovered for 5 minutes. Cover and cook until tender, 15-20 minutes longer and drain. Add a pinch of ground ginger to cooked or canned beans to eliminate gas problems.

TO MICROWAVE: Cover and microwave lima beans and 1/2 C water for 6 minutes; stir. Cover and microwave until tender, 4-6 minutes more. Let stand 1 minute, then drain, season and serve. **Seasonings good with limas beans are lemon, garlic, and oregano.**

9 PERKY LIMA BEANS

2 C shelled fresh lima beans*
2 T margarine, softened
1 t sugar
1 t dry mustard
1 t lemon juice
1/4 t salt

Cook beans in salted, boiling water or cook in a steamer to desired tenderness. Stir in remaining ingredients. Serves 4.
*1, 15-oz can drained lima beans, or 10-oz pkg frozen baby lima beans may be substituted.

10 CREOLE LIMA BEANS

Try a dash of Cayenne if you like it hot

2 C stewed tomatoes
2 C shelled fresh lima beans (or 1, 10-oz pkg frozen lima beans)
1 large stalk celery, chopped
salt and pepper to taste

Heat tomatoes to boiling. Stir in remaining ingredients. Return to boiling and reduce heat. Cover and simmer until beans are tender. Serves 5.

11 LIMA LUNCHEON

2 C fresh or 1, 10 oz pkg frozen lima beans
1 can cream of celery soup
1/2 C milk
2 T minced onion
seasonings to taste
3 hard boiled eggs
6 slices toast

Place raw or unthawed beans in a skillet. (An eletric skillet is good for this.) Add soup, milk, onion and seasonings. Cover and cook over low heat until beans are tender, about 35-40 minutes, stirring occasionally and adding water if necessary. Remove from heat and add sliced eggs. Serve immediately over toast. Serves 4-6.

is for Beets

Beets, which might seem to be unlovely root vegetables, are buried treasures. The greens of young tender beets are a seasonal treat for greens lovers; cook both the purple stem and green leaves and season with a touch of vinegar, salt and pepper. Scrub beets and cook without peeling, leaving a stub of stem on the beet to prevent "bleeding." Cook beets of approximately the same size in boiling water until fork tender. Cool, and you can easily slip the smooth, deep red beauties from their skins. (Wear rubber gloves for this. There is good reason that dyes have been made from beet juice.) Now they are ready to fix in dozens of ways. *Season beets with allspice, bay leaves, caraway seed, cloves, and ginger.*

12 BEETS AND PINEAPPLE

2 C beets, cooked
1/2 C brown sugar
2 T cornstarch
1/2 t salt
2 T vinegar

1 C water or beet juice
1/2 C raisins
2 T butter
1 C crushed pineapple
　undrained

Mix sugar, cornstarch and salt; stir in vinegar and add 1 C liquid slowly. Add raisins, butter and pineapple and cook slowly. Add beets and heat through.

13   BEETS IN SOUR CREAM

5 fresh medium beets, cooked and cut into julienne strips*
2 T margarine
2 t flour
2 T vinegar
1 T sugar
1/4 t salt
1/8 t pepper
1/4 t dried dill weed
1/2 C dairy sour cream
3 T milk

*1, 16-oz can drained shoestring beets may be substituted

Melt margarine and blend in flour. Cook over low heat, stirring constantly, until mixture is smooth and bubbly. Remove from heat and stir in vinegar, sugar, salt, pepper and dill weed. Return to heat and cook for 1 minute. Stir in beets and heat through. Blend sour cream and milk; add to beet mixture and heat just until hot. Do not boil. Serves 4.

14 GARDEN BORSCHT

Besides beets, potatoes, carrots, rutabaga and cabbage!

6 C water or bouillon
1 medium onion, chopped
1 bay leaf
salt and pepper
1 medium rutabaga, diced
3 C cooked, diced beets
2 C celery, sliced
1 small head cabbage, shredded
2 1/2 C diced carrots
2 1/2 C diced potato
3/4 C pearl barley
2 C diced tomato
1/4 C vinegar
sour cream for garnish

Combine all ingredients except tomato, vinegar and sour cream and cook for about 45 minutes. Stir in tomatoes and vinegar. Cook 15 minutes more and adjust seasonings to taste. Ladle into bowls and top with a dab of sour cream.

15 ORANGE GLAZED BEETS

Tangy and pretty

3 T butter
1/4 C orange marmalade
1 T orange juice
2 C cooked or canned beets.

Melt butter; stir in marmalade and juice. Add beets. Cook and stir over low heat until beets are hot and glazed, about 6-8 minutes. Serves 4.

16 PICKLED BEETS

Great with sandwiches for lunch

4 C whole or sliced beets
1 1/2 C vinegar
1/2 C water or beet juice
2 C sugar
1 t mixed pickling spice
1 t salt

Drain beets, reserving juice; combine remaining ingredients and heat drained beets in the syrup until boiling. Simmer for 5 minutes. Cool and refrigerate. Serve with sandwiches or cottage cheese. These keep indefinitely.

is for Broccoli

What a versatile vegetable! Raw, its great with dips and in salads; cooked, its good with cheese sauce over toast or baked potatoes. Toss leftovers in soups casseroles. Especially good with egg dishes. *Seasonings good with broccoli are caraway seed, dill, and mustard.*

17 BROCCOLI POTATO SOUP

1/2 C chopped onion
2 T margarine
2 C water
1 t salt
2 C diced potato

2 C diced broccoli
1, 13 oz can evaporated milk
1 t Worcestershire sauce
1 1/2 C shredded cheese

Cook onion in margarine until soft, but not brown; add water, salt, potatoes and broccoli and cook until vegetables are tender. Add milk and Worcestershire sauce and heat. Melt cheese into mixture, but do not boil. Serves 4-5.

18 MARINATED BROCCOLI SALAD

10-16 oz broccoli pieces, cooked and cooled
1, 8 oz can mushrooms,
1, 6 oz can water chestnuts
2 C cherry tomatoes
1 C sliced ripe olives,
4 stalks celery, cut in 1/4 inch strips
1 large green pepper, cut in strips
1 bunch fresh green onions, sliced
1, 8 oz bottle Italian dressing

Mix in large bowl, cover and refrigerate several hours or overnight.

19 GARDENER'S SPECIAL

Start to finish in the microwave

1 head broccoli
1/2 head cauliflower
2 medium summer squash
3 T butter
1/2 t garlic salt
1/4 t thyme
2 tomatoes
1/4 C Parmesan cheese

Arrange cauliflower and broccoli pieces in a circle around outside of a serving dish or platter; slice squash in the center and cover all with plastic wrap. Cook 7 minutes on high or until vegetables are just about tender. Uncover and add tomato wedges. Melt butter and add garlic salt and thyme; drizzle over vegetables. Sprinkle with Parmesan and cook uncovered for 1 1/2 -2 minutes.

20   BROCCOLI WITH MUSTARD SAUCE

1 1/2 lb fresh broccoli
1 T butter
1 T half-and-half
1/2 t dry mustard
1 t sugar
1/8 t pepper

Cut and cook broccoli in boiling water for 12-15 minutes, or just until tender. Melt margarine, mix in remaining ingredients and pour over broccoli. Serves 4.

21   BROCCOLI AND RICE CASSEROLE

1 lg bunch fresh broccoli
1 1/2 C cooked rice
1 T margarine
1/4 C chopped onion
1 can cream of mushroom soup
1/2 C milk
4-8 oz shredded cheese
salt, pepper and paprika to taste
bread or cracker crumbs

Cook broccoli until just tender, drain and place in a greased casserole. Sauté onions in margarine, add to rice and pour over broccoli. Combine soup, milk, cheese and seasonings and pour over broccoli. Top with bread or cracker crumbs. Bake at 350° for 25 minutes. Serves 4-6.

22 CREAM CHEESE AND BROCCOLI

Delicious creamy sauce

1 1/2 lbs fresh broccoli or
   20 oz frozen broccoli cuts
1 medium onion, chopped
6 T margarine, melted
2 T flour
1 C milk

1, 8 oz pkg cream cheese
1/2 t salt
pepper to taste
1/2 C shredded yellow cheese
1 C bread crumbs
2 T margarine

Cook broccoli until just tender crisp and place in a buttered casserole. Sauté onion in margarine; stir in flour until mixture is smooth. Stir in milk, salt and pepper and cook until thickened. Cut cream cheese into chunks and add to hot sauce, stirring until melted. Pour cheese sauce over broccoli and sprinkle top with yellow cheese. Bake for 25 minutes at 350°. Brown bread crumbs in 2 tablespoons margarine and sprinkle over casserole. Bake 10 minutes more.

23 BROCCOLI WITH HERB STUFFING

20 ozs frozen broccoli cuts
1 egg, slightly beaten
1/2 C mayonnaise
1 small onion, chopped
1 can cream of mushroom soup
1 1/2 C shredded Cheddar cheese
2 C herb seasoned croutons
1/4 C melted butter

Cook broccoli until tender crisp. Combine egg, mayonnaise, onion, soup and cheese; add broccoli. Pour mixture into a buttered 2 quart casserole. Mix croutons with butter and sprinkle over broccoli. Bake at 350° for 30 minutes.

24 BROCCOLI AND CAULIFLOWER BAKE

1 small head broccoli
1 small head cauliflower
3 eggs
1 C cottage cheese
1 C shredded Cheddar cheese
3 T flour
salt and pepper to taste

Break broccoli and cauliflower in pieces and steam until tender crisp. Mix remaining ingredients and stir in vegetables. Pour into a buttered casserole and bake at 350° for 30-35 minutes. Serves 6-8.

is for Brussels Sprouts

Rich in vitamin C, this vegetable is underused considering how versatile it is. Besides the favorite Hollandaise sauce, try mustard-cheese sauces, paprika and sour cream, browned butter and tomato sauces. Cook fresh sprouts in one inch of boiling water without a cover for 5 minutes, then cover and cook 10 minutes or until just tender. *Season Brussels sprouts with lemon, garlic and mustard.*

25 MICROWAVE HOLLANDAISE FOR SPROUTS

1/4 C butter
1 1/2 T lemon juice
1/4 C half and half

2 egg yolks
1/4 t salt
1/2 t dry mustard

Heat butter and lemon juice on *high* for 1 minute. Stir in half and half and egg yolks. Cook on *high* for 1 1/2 minutes, stirring every 15 seconds. Whip in salt and mustard. Cook on *medium* for 2 minutes. Makes 3/4 cup sauce. Pour sauce over hot cooked Brussels sprouts.

26 BRUSSELS SPROUTS WITH LEMON

Combine 1 pound fresh Brussels sprouts with 1/2 cup water. Cover and microwave on *high* for 4-8 minutes. Combine 2 tablespoons melted butter, 2 teaspoons fresh lemon juice, 1/2-1 teaspoon grated lemon rind, 1/2 teaspoon each garlic powder, salt and pepper. Pour over hot sprouts and serve.

is for Cabbage

Cut these beautiful, shiny green heads before they burst! Chop or shred and eat it raw or boiled, fried, wrapped around other foods, or in soup. To prevent room odor while cooking cabbage or cauliflower, put a bread crust on top of cabbage before putting on the lid of cooking pot and discard the bread after cooking or add 1 T lemon juice or a wedge of lemon with rind to cooking pot. *Season cabbage with caraway seed, vinegar, sour cream, lemon and dill.*

27   EVER READY COLD SLAW

Salad always ready to serve.

1 medium head cabbage
3-4 carrots
2 red peppers
2 green peppers
2 large onions
1/3 C salt

water to cover
2 C white vinegar
2 1/2 C sugar
2 t celery seed
2 t dry mustard

Grind or chop vegetables and sprinkle with salt; cover with water and soak for 2 hours. Heat vinegar and sugar together, stirring until sugar dissolves, but do not boil; add celery seed and mustard. Cool syrup. Drain salt water from vegetables and place in a non-metallic container. Pour on cooled syrup. Cover and let stand in refrigerator. Store in glass jars in refrigerator or freezer. Ready to serve after 24 hours.

28 JUST GREAT CABBAGE SALAD

A cabbage lovers favorite

5 C shredded cabbage
3/4 C shredded carrot
1/2 C chopped green pepper
1/4 C minced onion

1/2 C salad dressing
1-2 T vinegar
1 T sugar
salt and pepper to taste

Combine cabbage, green peppers, carrots and onions in large bowl. Combine salad dressing, vinegar, sugar, salt and pepper and thin with a little mik. Add to cabbage mixture and toss lightly.

29 CRUNCHY CABBAGE SALAD

Different and delicious

1 medium head cabbage, shredded
4 sliced green onions
1 pkg Ramen soup mix
Dressing:
3 T red wine vinegar
1/2 C salad oil

1 T sugar
salt to taste
1/2 t pepper

1/2 C sliced almonds
2 T sesame seeds

Shred cabbage very finely and add sliced onions. Toast almonds and

sesame seeds in a skillet until lightly browned stirring constantly. Mix dressing ingredients and add seasonings from packet in soup mix; pour over cabbage and toss well. Refrigerate until serving time. At serving time, crush dry noodles and toss with salad. Add toasted seeds and almonds. Serves 8.

30 MIXED UP CRUNCHY CABBAGE SALAD
A wonderful summer salad

4 C shredded cabbage
1 C thinly sliced celery
1/2 C sliced radishes
1/2 C mayonnaise
1/2 C sour cream
1 t salt

1/4 C chopped green pepper
1/2 C diced cucumber
1/2 C sliced green onion
1/2 C dry roasted peanuts
1 T butter
2 T Parmesan cheese

Combine cabbage, celery and radishes and chill. Combine mayonnaise, sour cream, salt, green pepper, cucumber and onion; cover and chill. Just before serving, brown peanuts lightly in butter and add Parmesan cheese. Toss vegetables with dressing, place in a salad bowl and sprinkle nut and cheese mixture on top.

31 CABBAGE STIR-FRY

1 lb fresh mushrooms
1 large onion
1 large red or green pepper
1 large head cabbage, shredded

2 T olive oil
pepper and nutmeg to taste
1/2 t caraway seeds
1/4 C soy sauce

Slice mushrooms, onion and pepper. Heat oil in wok or large frying pan; add onion, caraway seeds, soy sauce and other spices. Continue to stir and add vegetables. Stir fry an additional 4-5 minutes or until cabbage and pepper are almost wilted. Serve over rice, noodles or by itself. Serves 6-10.

32 FRIED CABBAGE WITH SOUR CREAM

Quick and delicious for lunch with a muffin

1/2 head shredded cabbage
2 T butter or margarine

1/3-1/2 C cultured sour cream
salt and pepper to taste

Fry cabbage in butter until slightly browned; season to taste. Mix sour cream lightly into cabbage and heat just until hot. Serves 4.

33 SWEET & SOUR CABBAGE

Red cabbage is especially nice

5 C cabbage, shredded
2 T olive oil
2 T brown sugar
2 T flour

1 small onion, diced
1/2 C water
1/3 C vinegar
salt and pepper

Cook cabbage in boiling water for 7 minutes and drain. Heat oil, add sugar and flour and cook until blended. Add water, vinegar and seasonings to taste; cook until thickened. Add cabbage and chopped onion to sauce. Heat just until hot. Serves 4-6.

34 FRIED CABBAGE WITH APPLE

2 T olive oil
4 C shredded cabbage
2 C cubed unpeeled apple
1/4 C brown sugar

1/4 C vinegar
salt and pepper to taste
1/2 t caraway seed
1/4 C water

Heat oil in skillet and add remaining ingredients. Cook covered over low heat, stirring occasionally. For crisp cabbage, cook 15 minutes; for tender, 25-30 minutes. Serves 4-5.

C is for Carrots

Carrots are a naturally sweet vegetable often used in desserts and can be cooked dozens of ways. They may be boiled with the skins on, then the skins will slip off just like a beet skin. Besides being chopped, sliced and shredded raw, they may be fried, baked, broiled and boiled. Try boiling with potatoes and then mash together for a new color and flavor for dinner. *Seasonings good with carrots are molasses, allspice, cinnamon, ginger, and nutmeg.*

35 SWEET AND SOUR CARROTS

1 lb carrots
1 medium onion, sliced
1 1/2 C sliced celery
1 bell pepper, sliced
1 C tomato soup

1/2 C vinegar
1/2 C salad oil
1/2 C sugar
1 t Worcestershire sauce
1 t soy sauce
1/2 t salt

Scrape carrots and slice 1/4 inch thick; steam until just tender. Place onion, pepper and celery over carrots. Combine remaining ingredients and heat until sugar is dissolved. Pour hot mixture over vegetables. Marinate for 24 hours before serving.

36 CARROTS WITH ORANGE

5 medium carrots
1 T sugar
1 t cornstarch
1/4 t ground ginger

1/4 t salt
1/4 C orange juice
2 T butter

Cut carrots into 1 inch chunks. Cook in boiling water until just tender and drain. In saucepan, mix sugar, cornstarch, ginger and salt. Add juice and cook until thickened. Stir in butter and toss with carrots. Serves 4.

37 KITTY'S CARROT SALAD

Unusual and always a hit

3 C shredded carrot
1 small onion, minced
1 C frozen baby peas
1, 6 1/2 oz can white tuna
3/4-1 1/4 C salad dressing

1 t vinegar
2 t sugar
1 t salt
1 small can french fried
   potato sticks

Mix carrot, onion, peas and tuna. Stir in salad dressing until mixture is moistened, but not too moist. Season with vinegar, sugar and salt. Just before serving, add potato sticks and toss lightly. Serves 8-10.

38 CARROT AND HORSERADISH CASSEROLE

8 medium carrots
1/2 C mayonnaise
2 T finely chopped onion

2 T horseradish
salt and pepper to taste
1/3 C bread crumbs

Slice carrots and cook until tender; drain and cool. Combine with remaining ingredients and bake at 350° for 15 minutes. Serves 4.

39 CARROT BAKE

Wrap in foil and pop in the oven or on the grill

8 carrots
1/2 C chopped onion
1/2 C raisins

1 apple, cored and cubed
2 T honey
2 T sunflower seeds

Scrub carrots and cut in strips. Spray a large sheet of foil and place carrots on bottom; add all other ingredients and fold tightly into a package. Bake at 375° for 40 minutes or grill for about the same amount of time, turning package occasionally on grill.

40 CARROT BREAD

Bake in bread pan, or in tin cans for moist round slices

2 C flour
2 t soda
2 t cinnamon
1/2 t salt
1 1/3 C sugar
1/2 C currants

1/2 C chopped pecans
2/3 C oil
2 t vanilla
3 eggs
2 C grated carrots

Combine dry ingredients and stir in currants and nuts. Stir in remaining ingredients just until blended. Pour into one greased bread pan or into three greased #2 size cans. Bake at 350° for 1 hour, or less for tin cans. Cool slightly and remove from pan or cans. Cool, wrap in plastic wrap and refrigerate to store.

41 DOROTHY'S 14-KARAT CAKE

2 C flour
2 t baking powder
2 t cinnamon
1 1/2 t soda
1 1/2 t salt
1 2/3 C sugar

1 1/3 C vegetable oil
4 eggs
2 1/2 C grated carrots
1/2 C nuts
1 C crushed pineapple
3 1/2 oz coconut (optional)

Combine dry ingredients. Add oil and eggs and mix thoroughly. Drain pineapple and add with remaining ingredients to batter. Pour into a greased 9x13 inch pan or 3, 9-inch layers and bake at 350° for 35-40 minutes. Frost with cream cheese frosting.

Cream Cheese Frosting:
2, 3 oz pkgs cream cheese
1/4 C butter
1 t vanilla
1 lb powdered sugar
Cream cheese and butter together until smooth; add sugar and vanilla and a few drops of milk to thin to spreading consistency.

is for Cauliflower

These beautiful white heads are pretty enough to use as centerpieces. Cook the whole head at once or the flowerlets separately. Cook and use half cauliflower with half potatoes in potato salad; slice or chop and eat raw in salads. **Herbs and spices for cauliflower: Caraway seed, celery salt, dill, mace or curry.**

42 CREAMY CAULIFLOWER SOUP

1 medium head cauliflower, chopped
2 C water
1 large stalk celery, sliced
1 medium onion, chopped
1 T lemon juice
2 T margarine

2 T flour
2 1/2 C water
1 T bouillon
 salt and pepper to taste
1/4 t ground nutmeg
1/2 C whipping cream

Combine 2 C water, cauliflower, celery, onion and lemon juice. Cover and cook until tender, about 10 minutes; do not drain. Mash or purée mixture until of uniform consistency. Melt margarine and stir in flour; cook, stirring constantly, until mixture is smooth and bubbly. Stir in 2 1/2 C water, heat to boiling and cook for 1 minute. Stir in cauliflower mixture, bouillon, and seasonings. Return to boiling and stir in cream; heat but do not boil. Serve with shredded sharp cheese if desired. Serves 8.

43 MARINATED CAULIFLOWER SALAD

Tossed salad of a different nature

4 C thinly sliced cauliflower
1/2 C chopped ripe olives
1 green pepper, sliced
1/2 red pepper, sliced
1/2 C chopped onion
1/2 C vegetable oil
3 T lemon juice
3 T red wine vinegar
salt, pepper and sugar to taste

Combine vegetables in a deep bowl. Combine remaining ingredients, mix and pour over vegetables. Toss well and refrigerate at least 4 hours. Toss again before serving.

44 PINK CAULIFLOWER SALAD

On a diet? Fill up on this tasty business

2 C sliced raw cauliflower
2 C diced cooked beets
1/3 C diced onion
1 C sliced celery
1, 6 1/2 oz can water packed tuna
salt, pepper and herbs of choice
fat free salad dressing of choice

Combine ingredients and chill to blend flavors. Serves 2.

45 CREAMY CAULIFLOWER SALAD

1 head cauliflower
1 1/2 C cooked peas
1/2 C shredded cheese
1 pkg dry Italian salad
  dressing mix
1 C salad dressing

Cut cauliflower in bite-sized pieces. Combine cauliflower, peas and cheese. Stir dry dressing mix into salad dressing and mix lightly with vegetables. Cover and chill for 24 hours.

46 GARDEN IN A DISH

Is this healthy eating or what?

3 C cauliflower, broken in pieces
1 lb carrots, sliced
1 lb broccoli, broken in pieces
1 C mayonnaise
1/4 C onion
3 T horseradish
1/4 t salt
1/8 t pepper
1/2 C dry bread crumbs
2 T butter
1/2 t paprika

Cook cauliflower and carrots, covered, in a little water for 5 minutes. Add broccoli and cook 5 more minutes or until crisp-tender. Drain vegetables and place in a greased casserole. Combine mayonnaise, onion, horseradish, salt and pepper and pour over vegetables. Combine bread crumbs, butter and paprika and sprinkle over all. Bake uncovered for 15 minutes at 350° or until heated through and topping is golden. Serves 8-10.

47 CAROL'S CURRIED CAULIFLOWER

A vegetarian's favorite recipe

1 large head cauliflower
1 can cream of mushroom soup
1 C shredded Cheddar cheese
1/2 C mayonnaise
1 t curry powder
1/4 C bread crumbs

Break cauliflower in pieces and steam until just tender; place in a buttered baking dish. Mix soup, cheese, mayonnaise and curry powder and pour over cauliflower. Sprinkle with crumbs. Bake at 350° for 30 minutes.

48 CAULIFLOWER IN SOUR CREAM SAUCE

1 medium head cauliflower
1/4 C butter
2 T flour
1/2 t each salt and dry mustard
2/3 C milk
1 C sliced fresh mushrooms
1/2 sliced green onion
1/2 C sour cream

Remove part of core and cook whole cauliflower head in covered pan in 3/4 inch water for 20-25 minutes. Melt butter and stir in flour and seasonings until smooth; add remaining ingredients except cream and cook for 1 minute. Stir in cream and heat but do not boil. Place whole cauliflower head on a platter and pour sauce over it. Serves 6.

is for Corn

Boil, bake and grill it, on the cob or off. Can, freeze or dry it for soups. Everyone, including raccoons, loves corn except maybe the kid with front teeth missing. To cook on top of stove, drop husked ears in boiling water, cover and cook 5-6 minutes or until milk is set. Bake an ovenful by placing ears on squares of foil add butter, salt and pepper, seal well and bake at 425° for 20-25 minutes. To grill, pull back husks, remove silk, replace husks and grill for 20-25 minutes, turning to cook evenly. Wrap ears in plastic wrap and microwave for about 3 minutes per ear.

49 ORIENTAL CORN SOUP

2 T oil
1 C minced onion
1 clove garlic
6 C vegetable broth
2 C whole kernel corn
1 t each ground ginger and sugar

1/4 t pepper
2 T soy sauce
2 T water
1 T cornstarch
2 eggs
2 green onions, sliced

Sauté onion and garlic in oil; add broth and bring to a boil. Stir in corn, and seasonings and heat until hot. Combine soy sauce, water and cornstarch and stir into hot mixture, stirring until thickened. Beat eggs in a bowl with a whip and stir in onions. Gradually stir egg mixture into soup, stirring until eggs are just set. Serve with additional soy sauce.

50 CORN AND RICE SALAD

Great color and flavor

2 C canned whole kernel corn
2 C cooked rice
1/4 C chopped sweet pepper
1/4 C sliced green onion
1/4 C ripe olives
3 T vinegar
2 T soy sauce
2 T snipped parsley, or 1 T dried
1/2 t Dijon mustard
1/4 t garlic powder
1 1/2 C diced tomatoes
1 T Parmesan cheese

Combine ingredients and mix well. Cover and chill for several hours. Serves 8.

51 MEXICAN SALAD BOWL

Quick to put together for lunch

1/2 C mayonnaise
1/4 C minced green onion
2 T chili sauce
2 t vinegar
1 t onion salt
1/2 t chili powder
4 drops hot pepper sauce
2 C whole kernel corn
1, 15 oz can red kidney beans
1/2 C sliced black olives

Drain beans and corn well. Mix first seven ingredients; add corn, beans and olives to dressing and stir to blend. Chill. Serves 6.

52 SCALLOPED CORN

There are dozens of variations of this old favorite

1 small green pepper, diced
1 small onion, diced
1 T butter
2 T flour
1 t salt
1/2 t paprika
1/4 t dry mustard
1 C milk
2 C whole kernel corn
1 egg
1/2 C bread cubes
1 T melted butter
cracker crumbs

Sauté pepper and onion in butter; stir in flour and seasonings. Add milk gradually, stirring constantly and bring to the boiling point. Brown bread cubes in butter and add with corn and egg to mixture. Pour into a buttered casserole dish and top with cracker crumbs. Bake at 375° for 30-40 minutes or until set in center. Serves 6.

53 DOUBLE CORN CASSEROLE

Fresh corn, and corn meal as a thickener

1 1/2 C fresh whole kernel corn
1/2 C chopped onion
1/2 C chopped green pepper
1/2 C water
1 C chopped summer squash
1 large tomato, chopped

2/3 C cornmeal
1/2 C milk
2 eggs
salt and pepper to taste
hot pepper sauce to taste
3/4 C shredded cheese

Combine corn, onion and green pepper with water and cook for 5 minutes; do not drain. In a large buttered casserole combine remaining ingredients; add cooked vegetables and mix well. Bake uncovered at 350° for 40-45 minutes. Garnish with tomato and pepper slices. Serves 6-8.

54   QUICK CORN PUDDING

In the oven or microwave; out of this world with fresh corn

1/2 C butter
1/4 C sugar
3 T flour
1/2 C evaporated milk

2 eggs, beaten
1 1/2 t baking powder
2 1/2 C whole kernel corn,
   fresh, frozen or canned

Melt butter, remove from heat and stir in sugar and flour; add milk, eggs and baking powder, mixing well. Stir in corn. Pour into a 2 quart buttered casserole and Bake at 350° about 45 minutes, or until set and top is golden. For microwave, cook on high for 10-15 minutes. Can be baked in custard cups for individual servings. Serves 6-8.

55   FIVE MINUTE CORN RELISH

Serve it chilled with sandwiches

2 C whole kernel corn
1/3 C water
2 T chopped pimiento
1/4 C pickle relish

1 T brown sugar
1 T vinegar
2 t prepared mustard
1/2 t salt

Combine ingredients and simmer for 5 minutes. Chill.

is for Cucumbers

In a salad, or a salad by themselves, cucumbers add crunch and flavor every time. Fix them with sour cream and onions. Slice, marinate in vinegar and water, add sliced onion, salt and lots of black pepper. Make cold soups, or leave peel on and heap slices with any number of egg or cheese spreads for appetizers. **Season cucumbers with black pepper, basil, dill and mint.**

56 CREAMY CUCUMBER SOUP

Cool and luscious; try pretty garnishes

2 T butter
1/2 C sliced green onions
2 C diced cucumber
1 C chopped raw spinach
1/2 C peeled, diced potato
2 C bouillon
3/4 t salt
1 C heavy (or light) cream

Cook onion, including tops, in butter until tender, but not browned; add all other ingredients except cream and simmer for 15 minutes. Cool slightly and purée in blender in small batches. Put mixture in a large non-metallic bowl and stir in cream; cover and chill thoroughly for several hours or overnight. Serve cold and float garnishes on cups of soup; a thin slice of cucumber with a sprinkle of curry powder, thin radish slices overlapped, sliced green onion tops, parsley etc.

57 CUCUMBER DRESSING SUPREME

Keep on hand to spoon over crisp cucumber slices

1 C sugar
1 T flour
1 egg
1 T butter
1/2 C vinegar
1/2 C water
salt and pepper to taste

Beat egg and combine with other ingredients; cook until thickened and chill. Serve cold over cucumbers. Makes 1 1/2 C dressing.

58 MOLDED CUCUMBER SALAD

A tangy salad to serve with ham

1 lb cottage cheese
1/2 C salad dressing
1 t vinegar
1 small onion, finely diced
1 medium unpeeled cucumber
1 pkg lemon gelatin
1/2 C boiling water

Prepare vegetables and mix with cheese, salad dressing and vinegar. Dissolve gelatin in water and immediately stir in cheese mixture. Pour into a flat serving dish or greased mold and chill until set. Serves 6.

is for Dandelions

I've never seen a garden or yard without some dandelions, have you? When you have lemons, make lemonade. Or in this case, eat those little devils. The greens are very dark green when cooked and have a distinctive meaty flavor. Once you've eaten them, you'll look forward to a mess of dandelion greens every spring. Any greens such as collard, mustard, beet, and turnip greens, spinach and chard are good with this sour cream and egg dressing.

59 DANDELION GREENS

Cut tender young greens at ground level cutting off root. Gather them before they flower although those with small buds are fine. Wash in salt water, and under running water, to remove grit. If you pick your greens on sandy soil instead of in black dirt the larger grains of sand wash off more easily. Cook in a small amount of water until tender and drain.
Stir together:

1/2 C cultured sour cream
1 beaten egg

2 t vinegar
salt and pepper to taste

Pour over hot greens, cooking for a minute until egg is cooked and mixture looks slightly curdled. This amount of dressing is enough for approximately a pound of greens uncooked. Enjoy!

60 DANDELION WINE

The bees dont need all the nectar

5 lbs dandelion flowers
5 lbs sugar
2 pkgs dry yeast
water

Pick full flowers that have not been sprayed. Wash flowers then place in a large saucepan and bring to a full boil. Remove from heat and add sugar, stirring to dissolve; cool to lukewarm and add yeast. Place mixture in a crock and cover with a towel. Let stand for 15 days. Scoop off dandelions with a slotted spoon. Taste and add more sugar if desired. Let stand, covered for 15 days more. Taste for alcoholic content. If not strong enough, add more sugar and bottle.

E is for Eggplant

Besides being beautiful with its dark purple skin, egg plant is a low calorie and versatile vegetable. Use it for a centerpiece or as a base for appetizers on toothpicks. Fry slices in butter, breaded or not breaded; stuff it with any number of stuffings or make into scalloped dishes. It is a tropical type plant that needs to be used soon after it is harvested for best quality. *Seasonings for eggplant are marjoram and oregano.*

61   SCALLOPED EGGPLANT

Tastes something like scalloped oysters

1 medium eggplant
1 small onion, chopped
1 egg, beaten
1/2 C milk
2 T butter
1 C dry bread crumbs
salt, pepper and seasonings to taste
2 slices buttered bread

Peel eggplant and cut into cubes; cook in salted water for 8 minutes and drain. Combine eggplant with onion, egg, milk and dry bread crumbs; dot with butter. Butter two slices bread, cut into cubes and sprinkle over top. Bake uncovered at 350° for 30 minutes. Let stand 5-10 minutes before serving.

62 EGGPLANT ITALIAN

There are dozens of versions of this favorite. Fresh tomatoes or canned spaghetti sauce; more cheese and less cheese; to bread or not to bread the eggplant; have it your own way

3 lbs eggplant
1/4 C olive oil, approximately
3 lbs tomatoes
1 clove garlic, crushed
1/2 t salt
1/2 t basil
1/2 t oregano
1/3 C Parmesan cheese
2 lb Ricotta cheese
1 C mozzarella cheese

Peel eggplant and slice lengthwise in 1/4 inch slices; salt each slice and allow to drain for one hour. Wipe the slices dry with paper towels. Heat oil in fry pan and fry slices, a few at a time until golden. *Another method is to brush slices with oil and broil for several minutes on each side. Some cooks dip the dried eggplant in egg-milk wash and then in dry bread crumbs before frying.* Peel and squeeze fresh tomatoes to remove much of the juice, or if using canned, drain, chop and drain again. Purée tomatoes in a blender with salt, oregano and basil. *Canned spaghetti sauce may be substituted.* Mix Ricotta and Parmesan cheeses. Place half of tomato sauce in a buttered flat casserole; lay half of eggplant slices in sauce, spread with half of cheese mixture and repeat layers. Top with

mozzarella. Bake at 400° for 25-30 minutes.

*To microwave, before adding mozzarella, cover casserole with waxed paper and cook on high for 10 minutes; uncover, add mozzarella and cook uncovered for 7 minutes. Let stand 5-10 minutes before serving.

*One famous restaurant eliminates the Ricotta and uses a layer of sauce, layer of eggplant, layer of sliced mozzarella, sauce again, and tops it with Parmesan.

63 TUNA STUFFED EGGPLANT

2 large eggplants
1 small onion, chopped
1/4 C margarine
1 C soft bread crumbs
2, 7 oz cans tuna

1 t salt
1/2 t pepper
3/4 t thyme
1 C bread cubes
2 T melted butter

Wash and remove green tips from eggplants; cut a lengthwise slice from each one. Scoop out and reserve inside, leaving a 1/2 inch wall; invert shells in a baking pan, add 1 inch boiling water and bake at 400° for 20 minutes. Chop eggplant pulp and sauté with onion in margarine; add bread crumbs, tuna and seasonings. Spoon mixture into shells. Stir bread cubes in melted butter to coat and sprinkle over stuffed shells. Bake at 350° for 20 minutes. 4 Servings.

64 BAKED RATATOUILLE

The wonderful kitchen smells! Party fare in some places

2 C cubed summer squash
1 1/2 t salt
3 cloves garlic, minced
1/3 C oil
1/3 t cumin seed
2 C peeled, cubed egg plant

3/4 t oregano
3 medium onions, sliced
2 green peppers, sliced
1/2 t marjoram
3 medium tomatoes, sliced
1/3 t dill seed

Cover bottom of large, buttered casserole with squash cubes; sprinkle with 1/3 of the salt, garlic and oil and the cumin seed. Make a second layer with eggplant and 1/3 of salt, garlic and oil and the oregano. Place onion and pepper slices and remaining salt, garlic, oil and the marjoram. Cover dish and bake at 350° for 1 hour. Add sliced tomatoes and sprinkle with dill seed. Bake uncovered for 15 minutes. Serves 6.

is for Greens

There is a whole alphabet of soft greens to eat raw or cooked, to serve separately or mixed for added color and texture in salads. Some are grown just to use as greens, others are the tops of root vegetables, best eaten when small. Certain greens are more popular in different parts of the country, but all are generally a good source of vitamin A.

Bibb lettuce: Dark green in color; short leaves that form a compact head.
Beet greens: See #12.
Collards: Serve cooked.
Dandelion greens: See #59.
Escarole-Endive-Chicory: All the same species which add pleasing color and texture when used with other greens in salad. Endive has curly leaves; escarole usually has straight leaves.
Iceberg Lettuce: The common head lettuce, used for its crispness.
Kale: A member of the cabbage family. Good cooked, and its dark green leaves added to salad greens give a sweet distinctive flavor.
Leaf Lettuce: "Garden" lettuce that does not form a head. See #65.
Mustard Greens: Serve cooked.
Romaine: A lettuce with stiff upright leaves.
Spinach: See #113.
Swiss chard: Serve cooked.
Turnip Tops: Serve cooked.

is for Lettuce

The use of lettuce in sandwiches and salads is universal, but this green may also be wilted and cooked in both soups and main dishes. Also, try rolling any sandwich filling in a leaf of lettuce for an appetizer or a no-bread sandwich. **Herbs good in green salads are basil, chives, and dill.**

65 CREAM DRESSING FOR LEAF LETTUCE

The typical dressing for leaf lettuce

Mix together, 2 T sweet cream, 2 T sugar and 4 T vinegar. Wash and shake lettuce to remove moisture, or pat gently with a towel. Pour dressing over torn lettuce leaves and toss lightly.

66 UNUSUAL LETTUCE SALAD

Keep your family guessing about what's in it

1 C fine dry bread crumbs
3 T butter
10 C lettuce in bite-sized pieces
1 C mayonnaise
2 T Parmesan cheese
1 T lemon juice
1 clove garlic, minced
salt and pepper to taste
1-2 C grated cauliflower

Brown bread crumbs and cool. Break lettuce. Combine mayonnaise, cheese, lemon juice and garlic; season to taste with salt and pepper. Pour mixture over lettuce and toss well. Place salad in bowl and sprinkle first with crumbs and then with cauliflower. Serve immediately.

67 SEVEN LAYER SALAD

*Count this any way you like**

1 head lettuce, in bite sized pieces
1 C thinly sliced celery
1 small onion, chopped
1 green pepper, chopped
1, 10 oz pkg frozen peas
2 C shredded carrot
1 1/2-2 C salad dressing
2 T sugar
1 C shredded Cheddar cheese

Assemble salad in order given in container that may be used for serving. Peas may be added frozen. Use no salt. Mix sugar with dressing and spread salad dressing over peas with a spatula. Chill for 12 hours before serving. Serves 12.

*Additional or alternate layers: Chopped boiled egg, diced tomato, black olives, water chestnuts and chopped apple (which has been dipped in salt water to prevent browning).

68 ORIENTAL LETTUCE WITH EGG

An elegant stir-fried supper dish

Pancakes:
4 eggs
1 t salt
1 t sugar
1 t soy sauce
1 t oil

1 T oil
1/2 C sliced mushrooms
1 C sliced celery
4 C shredded lettuce
1/2 sliced green onion
sugar, salt and soy sauce to taste

Beat eggs with sugar and soy sauce. Heat 1 teaspoon oil in a non-stick fry pan and make four pancakes with egg mixture. Cool pancakes, roll together and cut like noodles. In fry pan or wok, heat 1 tablespoon oil and sauté mushrooms and diagonally sliced celery. Add lettuce and green onion; cook just until wilted. Season to taste with salt, sugar and soy sauce. Serve over rice.

is for Melon

This fruit, grown in most every garden, can be cubed and added to salads, can be used as a bowl *for* salad or ice cream, and can be pickled and kept for relish tray treats. What else can you take to a picnic and put in a lake to keep cool?

69   CANTALOUPE PICKLES

When you wish you could keep the golden beauties past summer
2 cantaloupes, sliced, seeded, peeled and diced

Bring fruit to the boiling point in 2 quarts of boiling water; drain.
For each cup of fruit use:
1/2 C brown sugar
1/4 C cider vinegar
1 t whole mace
1 t whole cloves
1 t broken cinnamon stick

Boil syrup for five minutes and pour over fruit in a large bowl. Ladle into sterilized jars and seal.

70   WATERMELON RIND PICKLES

You need melon with a thick rind for these. Raw rind may be covered with water and refrigerated for a day or two to accumulate enough, or plan ahead. Take a melon to a picnic or family reunion; collect the rind and take it home. Yes, you will be considered a little strange...until they taste your pickles.

6 # prepared melon rind
6 # white sugar
1 pint white vinegar
15 drops oil of cloves
15 drops oil of cinnamon

Peel rind and cut off any pink flesh; cut in bite-sized pieces. Cover the rind with cold water and bring to a boil; keep just under the boiling point for 12 minutes. Drain and rinse with cold water. Pour sugar over cooked melon and drop oils onto sugar. Pour on vinegar. Bring again to a boil and simmer for 7 minutes. Ladle into sterilized pint or half-pint jars and seal, or store in refrigerator indefinitely.

is for Okra

Develop a taste for okra and you'll have to grow this annual herb in your garden every year. Dry it to flavor soups and stews in winter by slicing fresh okra crosswise; thread on string with a long needle and hang to dry.

71 OKRA STEW

2 ears fresh corn
3/4 lb okra
3 T oil
1 medium onion, diced
1/2 green pepper, diced

2 stalks celery, diced
3-4 fresh tomatoes, diced
1 C cooked lima beans, drained
salt and pepper to taste
herb flavored croutons

Cut raw corn off cobs. Wash okra and slice crosswise. Cook onion, pepper and celery in oil until tender; add okra, tomatoes and beans. Cook for five minutes and add corn. cook for 12-15 minutes and season to taste. Serve over cooked rice with a few croutons.

72 CREAMED OKRA AND CORN

1/4 C butter
1/2 C fresh raw corn
2 C okra, cut in 1/2 inch pieces
1/2 C milk

1-2 T flour
salt and pepper to taste
2 T sliced ripe olives

Stir corn into melted butter and cook until it begins to brown; add okra, cover and cook on low for 10 minutes. Add milk and sprinkle with flour, stirring to thicken slightly. Season to taste and stir in olives just before serving.

73 OKRA PATTIES

A favorite from Georgia

2 C cooked okra
1 egg
1 t salt
4 T flour

2 T cornmeal
1/4 t black pepper
1/4 t baking powder
butter or oil for frying

Drain okra, mash well and add egg; mix well until blended. Mix dry ingredients together and add to okra. Drop by spoonsful into very hot butter or oil and fry until golden brown, turning only once.

is for onion

Onions should lobby for attention. True, they seem to be in most every mixture, but as the main ingredient, they are often overlooked. Onions can be stuffed, creamed and scalloped; made into soups and pies. But don't cry for the onion. Just hold onions under cold water to peel or hold a piece of bread crust or a clothespin in your mouth while peeling. To rid your hands, nails and cutting board of onion odors, rub with half a lemon or lime, or just the rind. In general, the larger the onion, the sweeter it is. *Season onions with caraway seed, mustard seed, nutmeg, oregano, sage or thyme.*

74 CHEESY SWEET ONION CASSEROLE

5-6 large sweet onions
1/2 C butter or margarine
4 T Parmesan cheese
1 1/2 C cracker crumbs
   (half cheese crackers)
salt and pepper to taste
1 can cream of mushroom soup
1 C shredded Cheddar cheese
1 t paprika

Sauté onions in butter. Layer half of onions in a buttered 1 1/2 quart casserole. Sprinkle with half of Parmesan and 3/4 cup cracker crumbs. Repeat layers with remaining onions, Parmesan and crackers. Spread undiluted soup and cheese over top. Sprinkle with paprika. Bake at 350° for 30 minutes. Serves 6.

75 DUTCH ONION RING SALAD

Serve this at your next barbecue

Dutch onion rings:
2 medium sweet onions
1/4 C dairy sour cream
1/4 t salt
1/2 t celery seed
1 t lemon juice

2-3 large tomatoes
1 small cucumber
Italian salad dressing
1/4 t salt
1/4 t black pepper
1/2 t dill seed
1 t snipped fresh parsley

Slice onions 1/4 inch thick; separate into rings and cover with boiling water. Let stand 2 minutes and drain. Chill onions. Before serving, combine sour cream, salt, celery seed and lemon juice; toss with onions. Slice tomatoes and cucumbers. Pile onions in center of a platter and border these with overlapping slices of tomatoes and cucumber; drizzle Italian dressing over slices, then sprinkle with salt, pepper, dill seed and parsley. Garnish platter with ripe olives. 6-8 servings.

76 DELUXE ONION PIE

Tempt your family with this

1 1/2 C thinly sliced onion
1/3 C butter
1 1/2 C cracker crumbs
1 t curry powder
1 C milk, scalded
1, 3 oz can mushrooms, drained

1/2 t salt
dash cayenne pepper
2 eggs, beaten
1 1/2 C shredded cheese

Cook onions in 2 tablespoons butter until transparent. Melt remaining butter and mix with cracker crumbs and curry powder. Line a 10 inch pie pan, or an 8x8 square pan with 1 cup of crumb mixture. Arrange cooked onions over crumbs. Combine milk, with remaining ingredients and mix well; pour over onions. Top with remaining crumbs. Bake at 350° for 30-35 minutes or until set. Serves 4-6.

is for Parsley

Fresh parsley will keep longer if you trim stems, put in a glass of water and refrigerate. Freeze parsley by washing the bunch, shake out moisture, secure with a rubber band and place in a plastic bag. To use, snip off desired amount with scissors. To dry parsley, trim off stems, plunge in boiling water for 30 seconds, spread on a screen and dry until crisp in a 300° oven with oven door ajar. Store in a tightly closed container.

77 PARSLEY AND RICE

An interesting twist in both ingredients and method

1 T oil
1 C rice
1 C finely chopped fresh parsley
1 t salt
2 1/2 C hot water

Brown rice slightly in oil in any oven proof glass covered container. Add water, parsley and salt. Cook over direct heat, covered for 3-4 minutes or until 1/2 of water is absorbed. Turn off burner and let stand on burner until all of water is absorbed. Serve hot.

78 TABBOULEH

A favorite salad from the middle east

1 1/4 C raw bulgar wheat*
4 C boiling water
3/4 C minced fresh parsley
3/4 C minced fresh mint leaves (some people use more)
3/4 C minced scallions
3 large tomatoes, seeded and chopped
3/4 C fresh lemon juice
1/4 C salad oil or olive oil
salt and pepper to taste

Pour boiling water over bulgar, turn off heat and let stand for 2 hours to soften. Drain very well so that water does not dilute flavors. Add remaining ingredients and let stand for several hours before serving.

*Bulgar comes in different sizes. #1 or small bulgar is sometimes not soaked in water before adding to salad, but salad must stand longer for bulgar to soften. #2 bulgar must be soaked.

is for parsnips

Use the same methods for using and storing parsnips as you do for carrots. They are good in stews, soups and mashed; cream them too. One traditional dish is to slice cooked parsnips lengthwise and sauté in butter.

79 PARSNIP CASSEROLE WITH ROSEMARY

12 parsnips, about 2 lbs
2 T butter
1/2 t dried rosemary
2 T flour
1/4 C Parmesan cheese
2 C half and half
1/2 C cracker crumbs
2 T melted butter

Peel parsnips and cook in boiling, salted water until tender; drain and cut in half lengthwise. Mix rosemary, flour and cheese. Arrange half of the parsnips in a greased baking dish; dot with a tablespoon of butter, sprinkle with half of dry mixture and drizzle with half of liquid. Repeat layers. Mix cracker crumbs with melted butter and sprinkle over casserole. Bake at 400° for 20 minutes.

is for Peas

Fresh peas should be cooked as soon after picking as possible as they deteriorate quickly in quality. They are an excellent source of many vitamins and minerals, especially iron. *Seasonings good with peas are garlic, basil, dill, marjoram, and mint.*

80   FRESH PEAS AT THEIR BEST

2 lbs peas in the pod
1 1/2 T butter
1 medium onion, sliced
1/4 t garlic powder
salt and pepper to taste

Shell peas, place in a sauce pan with water to cover and cook uncovered for 20 minutes, or until just tender. Drain. Sauté onion in butter until transparent; add peas and seasonings to taste, and serve immediately.

81   PEAS AND PEANUTS

1 C salted Spanish peanuts
1/4 C mayonnaise
1/4 C sour cream
1 C frozen peas
1 T lemon juice
1-2 t minced onion

Thaw and drain peas. Mix well with other ingredients and serve chilled.

82 SWEET-PEA RISOTTO

A foolproof microwave winner

1 T butter
1/3 C chopped onion
1 C short-grain rice
1 3/4 C broth
1/2 C white wine
3/4 C fresh green peas
1/4 C grated Parmesan
salt and pepper

In 2-quart microwave bowl, melt butter. Stir in onion, cover and cook for 1 minute. Add rice, mixing well; cover and cook for 1 minute. Stir in 1 cup broth and wine; cover tightly and cook for 6 minutes (rotate after 3 minutes if necessary). Stir in rice mixture, cover again and cook for 5-6 minutes. Stir in remaining 3/4 cup broth and the peas; cover and cook for 5-6 minutes or until rice is just cooked. Add Parmesan, pepper and salt, stirring until blended. Let risotto stand covered for 3 minutes before serving. Serves 4.

83 GREEN PEA CASSEROLE

1/2 C butter
1 C chopped onion
1/2 C sliced celery
1/2 C chopped green pepper
1 can cream of mushroom soup
1, 4 oz jar chopped pimiento
2 C cooked green peas, drained
1 C sliced water chestnuts

Melt butter in a skillet over low heat; add onion, celery and green pepper. Cook over low heat until vegetables are tender. Add remaining ingredients to vegetable mixture, stirring well. Pour mixture into a greased 1 1/2-2 quart casserole. Bake at 350° for 30 minutes. Serves 6-8.

84 CREAMED PEAS AND POTATOES

An every spring treat

2 C cubed potato
1 C fresh raw (or frozen) peas
3/4 C milk
1 1/2-2 T flour
1 T butter
salt and pepper to taste

Cook potatoes and peas together for 10-12 minutes or until tender; drain. Pour milk just to top of vegetables and sprinkle with flour, stirring just until thickened. Stir in butter, salt and pepper. Serve immediately.

is for Peppers

Cooked or raw, this vegetable can be stuffed with a variety of fillings. Try baking leftover casserole mixtures in pepper shells with a topping of cheese; stuff pepper quarters with cottage or creamed cheese mixtures for appetizers. Ground sweet red pepper, *paprika,* can be used in quantity for many sweet pepper flavored dishes.

85 SWEET RED PEPPER SOUP

This will be a new family favorite

1/4-1/3 C margarine
4 medium sweet red peppers
1 large onion, sliced
1 medium potato, diced

3 1/2 C vegetable broth
1/2 C milk
2 T lemon juice
2 green onions

Seed and slice peppers. Melt margarine and cook peppers and onion over low heat in a heavy pan for 20-30 minutes or until soft, adding more margarine if necessary. Add potato and broth and cook until potatoes are done. Purée mixture in batches and return to pan; stir in lemon juice and when mixed, add milk. Reheat. Soup should be the consistency of creamed soups. Slice onions and tops very thinly and sprinkle on top of each serving.

86 HOT SLAW STUFFED PEPPERS

Hot and spicy; if you don't like it hot, leave out Jalapenos

12 whole green peppers
4 qts water
1/4 C salt
2 medium heads cabbage
1/4 C salt (again)
1, 4 oz jar pimientos, diced
2-3 Jalapeno peppers, minced

6 C water
6 C cider vinegar
5 1/4 C sugar
1 1/2 whole cloves
5 sticks cinnamon
1 1/2 T whole allspice
1 1/2 t salt

Slice tops off peppers, save tops and remove seeds. Soak peppers and tops overnight in solution of 4 quarts water and 1/4 cup salt. Drain. Shred cabbage finely and sprinkle with 1/4 cup salt; let stand overnight then drain well. Mix pimientos and Jalapeno's with cabbage and stuff peppers. Tie tops on peppers with thread. Place stuffed peppers in an 8 quart crock. Combine water, vinegar, sugar and spices in sauce pan; bring to a boil and cook for 10 minutes. Pour hot solution over peppers and weight down with a plate. Marinate for at least one week. To serve, cut peppers in quarters. 12 peppers.

is for Potatoes

This vegetable is popular the world over and no wonder. It contains many nutrients, especially vitamin C. It is plentiful and inexpensive, and can be fixed countless ways. Cook an unpeeled potato in previously used deep fryer oil to absorb foreign flavors. Discard potato. *Season potatoes with garlic, basil, dill, chives, and oregano*

87 DILLED RED POTATO SALAD

Pretty red salad; leave the skins on

4 lbs small red potatoes
1 T vinegar
1 T oil
1 C minced red onion
salt and pepper to taste

1 C plain yogurt
1/2-1 C mayonnaise
1 T Dijon mustard
1-2 T dill weed

Cook and drain potatoes, cut in quarters, sprinkle with oil and vinegar and toss lightly to coat. Combine mayonnaise, yogurt and mustard and thin slightly with milk. Add mayonnaise mixture, onion, dill, salt and pepper to potatoes. Mix gently to coat well. Cover and chill before serving.

88 SOUR CREAM POTATO SALAD

Creamy dressing and cucumber for flavor

5 C cooked, diced potato
1/2 C finely diced cucumber
1 T minced onion
1 t celery seed
1 t prepared mustard

6 hard boiled eggs
1/2 C sour cream
1/2 C mayonnaise
2 T vinegar

Toss together potatoes, cucumber, onion, celery seed and salt. Remove yolks from eggs. Chop whites and add to potato mixture. Mash yolks with fork until fine and combine with sour cream, mayonnaise, vinegar and mustard. Fold dressing mixture into potatoes and chill. Serves 8.

89 POTATO CHOWDER WITH DUMPLINGS

4 C diced potato
1/2 C chopped onion
1 C shredded carrot
1 1/2 t seasoned salt

1 T dried parsley
6 C scalded milk
4 T butter

Combine vegetables, seasoned salt and parsley in a soup pot; add water to cover vegetables and cook for 15-20 minutes. Do not drain. Heat milk just to boiling point and add to soup. Drop dumplings onto soup, cover and simmer slowly for 10 minutes. Uncover and cook for an additional 10 minutes. Serves 6-8.

Dumplings: 1 C flour
1 1/2 t baking powder
1/2 t salt,
1/2 t sugar

1 t parsley flakes,
1 egg
1/2 C milk

Mix dry ingredients. Combine egg and milk and stir into dry ingredients until blended. Do not beat. Drop by spoonsful into chowder.

90 TWICE-BAKED POTATOES
Easier than most

8 medium baking potatoes
2 T butter
1/4 t salt

1 can Cheddar cheese soup
1 T chives

Bake potatoes until done. Cut potatoes in half lengthwise, scoop out insides leaving thin shell. Mash potatoes with butter and salt. Gradually add soup and chives; beat until light and fluffy. Spoon into shells. Sprinkle with paprika. Bake in shallow baking dish at 450° for 15 minutes or until hot. Serves 8.

91 MASHED POTATO CASSEROLE

10-12 medium potatoes
1 lb cottage cheese
1 C sour cream

salt and pepper to taste
1/4 C chives
1/4 C butter or margarine

Cook and mash potatoes; add remaining ingredients except butter. Place potatoes in a buttered casserole. Melt butter and pour on top. Bake at 350° for 25-30 minutes.

92 POTATO AND CARROT SKILLET

1 medium onion, sliced
3 T margarine
3 medium potatoes, sliced
2 medium carrots, sliced

1/2 t salt
1/4 t thyme
pepper to taste
1/3 C water

Sauté onions in margarine until soft. Add potatoes and carrots to skillet and stir until coated with margarine. Add seasonings and water; cover and cook over low heat for 20-25 minutes or until tender.

93 POTATOES AND CORN WITH BUTTERMILK

8 medium potatoes
4 ears fresh corn
2 T margarine
2 C buttermilk

1 C shredded cheese
salt and pepper to taste
chives

Peel and slice potatoes; cut corn off cobs. Layer half of potatoes in a buttered casserole; sprinkle with the corn. Dot with margarine and season to taste. Add the rest of the potato slices and pour buttermilk over all. Bake at 375° for 1 hour. Sprinkle with cheese and chopped chives and bake for 15 minutes more. Serves 8.

94 PARMESAN POTATOES

6 large potatoes
1/2 C flour
1/2 C Parmesan cheese

3/4 t salt
1/3 C butter
chopped parsley

Peel (or scrub) potatoes and cut into 4-6 wedges lengthwise. Mix flour, cheese and salt in a plastic bag. Shake potato pieces, a few at a time in flour mixture. Melt butter in a 13X9 pan and place potatoes in pan. Bake at 375° for 1 hour, turning once. Sprinkle with parsley. Serves 6-8.

95 POTATOES AND APPLES FOR TWO

To peel or not to peel; its up to you

2 small potatoes, cut in strips
1 medium apple, cubed
1 stalk celery
1/4 C chopped onion

1 T oil
salt and pepper
1/3 C shredded cheese

Heat oil in a skillet and add vegetables; season to taste. Cover and cook on low for 15-20 minutes. Sprinkle hot mixture with cheese and serve immediately.

96 POTATO CHOCOLATE CAKE

Makes two loaves; one for a neighbor

2/3 C shortening
2 C sugar
4 eggs
1 C hot mashed potato
1 t vanilla
1/2 C cocoa

2 C sifted flour
1/2 t salt
2 t baking powder
1 t cinnamon
1/2 t nutmeg
1 C buttermilk
1 C chopped nuts

Cream shortening and 1 1/2 cups sugar until light; beat in egg yolks. Stir in potatoes and vanilla. Sift dry ingredients and add alternately to creamed mixture with buttermilk. Beat egg whites, add remaining 1/2 cup sugar and beat until stiff; fold into cake batter with nuts. Pour into two 9X5 loaf pans and bake at 350° for 35-40 minutes or until cake tests done. Cool slightly and pour glaze over loaves.

Glaze: 3/4 C chocolate chips, 2 tablespoons butter. Melt together over low heat and spread on cakes.

is for Pumpkin

Pumpkins are a member of the squash family. Canned pumpkin is fairly in expensive, but yes, you can "do it yourself" from the garden and the fresh taste is different and interesting. Halve and then quarter pumpkin, remove seeds and stringy portion and cut in small pieces; cut off rind. Cook in lightly salted water for 25-30 minutes. Drain and mash. Place mashed pumpkin in a strainer and let excess liquid drain off.

97 PUMPKIN BREAD

A good bread to freeze

2 2/3 C sugar
4 eggs
2/3 C shortening
2 C pumpkin
3 1/3 C flour
1 1/2 t salt

1/2 t baking powder
2 t cinnamon
1/2 t cloves
2/3 C water
2/3 C nuts
2/3 C raisins or dates

Combine sugar, eggs, shortening and pumpkin. Stir dry ingredients together and add to creamed mixture alternately with water. Stir in nuts and fruit. Fill greased tin cans 1/2-2/3 full and bake at 350° for 1 hour.

98 PUMPKIN SQUARES

A brownie-type bar cookie to remember

1 1/2 C white sugar
2 C pumpkin
4 eggs
1/2 C oil

2 C flour
2 t soda
1 1/2 t cinnamon
1/2 t salt
1 C chopped nuts (optional)

Combine sugar, pumpkin, oil and eggs and mix well. Mix flour with remaining ingredients and stir into batter. Spread mixture in a greased jelly roll pan and bake at 350° for 15-20 minutes. Do not over bake. Cool and frost.

Icing: Combine 3 ozs cream cheese, 2 C powdered sugar, 6 T margarine, and 1 t vanilla with enough milk to spread.

99 FRESH PUMPKIN PIE WITH PECANS

A sweet treat labor of love

1 1/2 C mashed pumpkin
3/4 -1 C sugar
3 eggs
1 T flour
1 t ground ginger
1 t cinnamon
1/4 t nutmeg
1/8-1/4 t ground cloves
1/2 t salt
1 C milk or half and half
3/4 C chopped pecans (optional)
1, 9 inch unbaked pie shell

Mix all ingredients except pecans in order. Pour mixture into pie shell and sprinkle with pecans. Bake at 400° for 10 minutes; reduce heat to 350° and bake for additional 30 minutes or until knife inserted in center comes out clean.

100 PUMPKIN ROLL

Jelly roll cake with cream cheese filling

3 eggs
1 C sugar
1 t lemon juice
1 t soda
1/4 t salt
1 t ground ginger
1/2 t nutmeg
3/4 C flour
2/3 C cooked pumpkin
1 C chopped nuts
powdered sugar

Beat eggs until light; add sugar and lemon juice, beating well. Stir soda, salt and spices into flour and fold flour into batter until combined. Stir in pumpkin. Grease and line a jelly roll pan with waxed paper. Spread batter over paper and sprinkle with nuts. Bake at 375° for 20 minutes. Turn cake out onto a towel, remove paper and roll up, starting from the long side, rolling the towel into the loaf. Let cool. Unroll and spread with filling. Reroll filled cake and wrap in foil. Store in refrigerator until serving time.

Filling: Combine 1 cup powdered sugar, 8 ozs cream cheese, 4 tablespoons margarine and 1 teaspoon vanilla until smooth.

is for Rhubarb

The stalks of this perennial herb are best when crisp and tender, bright colored and medium sized. Rhubarb, sometimes called *pieplant,* has long been a pie bakers favorite, but you can make many other delicious things with it too! Besides the recipes here, it can be used in tarts, sauces, punch, jams and jellies. It is quickly and easily prepared, and can be washed, cut and stored in the freezer for winter treats.

101   RHUBARB SALAD

Salad? Dessert? Delicious!

8 C sliced rhubarb
1/4 C water
1 1/3 C sugar
1, 6 oz pkg strawberry gelatin

2, 10 oz pkgs frozen strawberries
   thawed, drained and reserve juice
3 C vanilla ice cream
2 T cornstarch
whipped cream or topping

Combine rhubarb and water; cover and simmer until tender, about 15 minutes. Remove from heat and stir in gelatin and sugar. Blend in drained fruit and ice cream.

Topping: Combine 1 cup reserved juice and cook with 2 tablespoons cornstarch until thick; cool. Whip and sweeten 1 cup whipping cream or use 2 cups whipped topping and fold into cooled juice. Serve over salad.

102   RHUBARB BREAD

A moist bread that freezes well

1 1/2 C brown sugar
2/3 C shortening
1 egg
1 C sour milk
1 t salt
1 t soda
1 t vanilla
2 1/2 C flour
1 1/2 C diced rhubarb
1/2 C nuts

Topping:
1 T butter
1/2 C sugar

Cream brown sugar and shortening; add egg and blend. Add combined dry ingredients and nuts alternately with milk. Stir in rhubarb. Pour batter into 2 greased bread pans. Mix topping ingredients and sprinkle over batter. Bake at 325° for 50-60 minutes. Do not overbake.

103   RHUBARB UP-SIDE-DOWN CAKE

3 T melted butter
2/3 C sugar
2 C cut-up rhubarb
1/2 C raisins

Melt butter in an 8X8 inch pan; add sugar, rhubarb and raisins.

Cake:
3 T melted butter
1/2 C sugar
1 egg
1 1/2 C flour
2 t baking powder
1/2 t salt
1/2 C milk

Mix butter, sugar and egg; add dry ingredients with milk and mix until smooth. Pour batter over topping in pan. Bake at 375° for 25 minutes. Invert pan. Serve with whipped cream or whipped topping.

104   RHUBARB PUDDING CAKE

Try various fruits and mixed fruits with this

2 C sliced fruit
3/4 C sugar
4 T margarine
1 C flour
1 t baking soda
1/2 C milk
1/2 t almond extract
1 C boiling water

Place rhubarb in a greased 8X8 inch pan. Cream sugar and margarine; mix flour and soda and stir into creamed mixture with milk and almond extract. Spread batter over fruit. Pour boiling water over batter. Bake at 325° for 50 minutes.

105 RHUBARB CRUNCH

A big dessert for a big family

Crust:
1 C flour
1 C brown sugar
1 t cinnamon
3/4 C quick oats
1/2 C butter

Mix until crumbly and spread half of mixture in bottom of a greased 13X9 pan.

Sauce:
4 C sliced rhubarb
2 T cornstarch
1 C water
1 C sugar
1 t vanilla

Cover and simmer 5-10 minutes. Pour sauce over crust in pan and top with remaining crust. Bake at 350° for 1 hour.

106 RHUBARB CUSTARD MERINGUE PIE

2 C sliced rhubarb
3 T water
3 egg yolks
2 T flour
3/4 -1 C sugar
1/2 t nutmeg
1 T butter
1 unbaked pie shell

Arrange rhubarb in pie shell; beat egg yolks with water and pour over fruit. Combine flour, sugar and nutmeg; spoon over fruit and dot with butter. Bake at 400° for 10 minutes, then at 350° for 35 minutes. Remove from oven and spread with meringue. Brown for 5-7 minutes. Watch closely.

Meringue: Beat 3 egg whites and 1/4 t cream of tartar until frothy; gradually beat in 6 tablespoons sugar and 1/2 t vanilla.

107 RHUBARB ORANGE CUSTARD PIE

Such a good blend of flavors

4 C sliced rhubarb
2 eggs, beaten
1/4 C orange juice
1 1/2 C sugar
3 T flour
1/4 t each salt and nutmeg
2 T butter
pastry for a two crust pie

Mix eggs, juice, sugar, flour, salt and nutmeg into rhubarb and pour into unbaked pie shell; dot with butter. Top with pastry cutouts, or lattice crust. Sprinkle crust with sugar. Bake at 400° for 10 minutes, then at 350° for 35 minutes more.

108 RHUBARB-APPLE PIES

6-8 large apples
5 C young rhubarb
2 C sugar
2 T flour

1 1/2 t nutmeg
1 1/2 t cloves
2-3 t cinnamon
pastry for 2, 9 inch pies

Cook rhubarb in a little water only until soft and drain well. Mix with rest of ingredients. Divide into 2, 9-inch unbaked pastry shells; top with lattice crusts and bake at 350° for 40-50 minutes.

109 STRAWBERRY RHUBARB PIE

Oh yes!

1 1/4 C sugar
1/4 t salt
1/3 C flour
pastry for two crust pie

2 C sliced rhubarb
2 C fresh strawberries
2 T butter

Combine sugar, salt and flour. Arrange half of the fruit in pie shell, sprinkle with half of sugar mixture; repeat with remaining fruit and sugar. Dot with butter. Put on a full or lattice crust and sprinkle top crust with sugar. Bake at 375° for 35-40 minutes.

is for Rutabaga

This root vegetable is like the turnip only larger, and with yellow flesh and skin. The rutabaga should be heavy in relation to size. It is usually cut up, boiled and mashed alone, or with other vegetables. Try cooked rutabaga with potatoes in salads. Cut it in strips and french fry, or use raw rutabaga sticks with apples in salad.

110 RUTABAGA CASSEROLE

A delicious new scalloped dish

1 small rutabaga, peeled and sliced
1 large potato, peeled and sliced
1 medium onion, peeled and sliced
1/2 C milk

2-3 T butter
salt and pepper
bread crumbs

Layer the three vegetables in a greased casserole, seasoning between layers. Pour milk over top and sprinkle with crumbs and dot with pieces of butter. Bake at 350° for 45 minutes or until potato and rutabaga are tender. Serves 4-6.

111 MASHED RUTABAGA

1 medium rutabaga
2 T butter or margarine
salt and pepper to taste

Peel and cut rutabaga in 1 inch cubes. Cook in salted water until tender. Drain most of water and mash with butter or margarine. Season to taste. Serves 4-6.

112 RUTABAGA AND CARROTS

A zesty touch of lemon

1 medium rutabaga
4-5 medium carrots
1/2 C water
2 T butter
3 T brown sugar (or to taste)

1 T lemon juice
1/2 t grated lemon rind
1/4 t salt
1/4 t dill weed

Cut carrots and rutabaga in narrow strips and cook in water until just tender and drain. Cook remaining ingredients for 2-3 minutes in a skillet and add cooked vegetables. Heat for a few minutes until vegetables are glazed.

is for Spinach

Spinach is one of the best liked greens. Cooked or raw, it is popular with gourmets, dieters and of course, Popeye. A good source of iron and Vitamin K and only 23 calories per serving! Wash spinach from the garden in salted water to remove dirt and sand faster. *Season spinach with vinegars, basil, marjoram, nutmeg or oregano.*

113 SPINACH OMELET APPETIZER

Cut in little squares or diamonds, or in larger pieces for a main dish

24 green onions
4 T butter
2 lbs spinach, chopped
1/3 C chopped parsley
12 eggs
1 1/2 t salt
1/2 t pepper
1/2 C sour cream
1 1/2 C shredded Swiss or Cheddar cheese
3/4 C Parmesan cheese

Clean and cut green onions in diagonal slices; sauté in butter until just tender. Add spinach and sauté for 2 minutes. Add parsley and set aside. Beat eggs until light. Stir in salt, pepper sour cream and shredded cheese; stir in 1/2 of the Parmesan cheese. Fold in spinach mixture and pour into a greased 15x10x1 inch jelly roll pan. Sprinkle with remaining Parmesan. Bake at 350° for 25 minutes or until set. Serve hot or cold.

114   BAKED SPINACH BALLS

Party fare that will be a hit

1, 10 oz pkg frozen chopped spinach
   or about 1 1/2 C cooked fresh spinach
1 C seasoned croutons
1/2 C Parmesan cheese
2 eggs, slightly beaten
1/4 C softened margarine
1/4 C minced onion

Drain cooked fresh spinach or thaw frozen spinach; no need to cook. Press as much moisture from spinach as possible with the back of a large spoon, then chop very fine. Crush croutons, and mix into spinach with remaining ingredients. Shape into balls the size of a walnut. Place on an ungreased baking sheet and bake at 350° for 10-12 minutes. Watch closely. 12-15 spinach balls. Recipe may be doubled.

115 SPINACH DIP

Serve in a loaf of bread

1 round loaf of crusty bread
2 lbs fresh or 2, 10 oz pkgs
   frozen chopped spinach
2, 8 oz pkgs cream cheese
1/4 C sliced green onion

1/2 t basil
1 t lemon juice
salt and pepper to taste
1 clove garlic, minced
1/8 t nutmeg

Cut a 1 1/2 inch piece off top of bread loaf and cut out the center of the loaf leaving a bread shell 2 inches thick on the bottom and 1 inch on sides. Cook and chop fresh spinach, or microwave frozen spinach *in the packages* for 4-6 minutes, turning over once. Drain spinach in a sieve and squeeze out as much moisture as possible. Heat cheese in microwave until soft; stir in spinach and remaining ingredients. Spoon spinach mixture into bread shell, place on paper towels and heat in microwave for about 1 minute until bread is warm. Serve with bread cubes for dipping.

116 SIMPLE SPINACH SALAD

A waitress shared the restaurant's "secret" dressing recipe

washed fresh spinach
sliced fresh mushrooms
sliced onion
sliced boiled egg
bottled celery seed dressing, warmed

117 CHEESE & SPINACH SALAD

Vegetarian spinach salad

Dressing:
3 T vinegar
1/2 C sour cream
2 T sugar
1 T horseradish
1/2 t dry mustard

1 lb fresh spinach
1 1/2 C creamed cottage cheese
1/2 C chopped walnuts

Combine dressing ingredients and chill. Trim stems and wash and drain spinach; arrange in salad bowl and top with cheese and nuts. Pour on dressing and toss to blend. Serves 8.

118 SPINACH AND MUSHROOM PASTA

A sauce that is good with many vegetables

2 C cream style cottage cheese
2, 3 oz pkgs cream cheese
1/2 C chopped onion
2 T butter or margarine
2 C chopped fresh mushrooms
1/3 C white wine

1/2 t dried thyme
salt and pepper to taste
2/3 C evaporated milk
2 C cooked spinach
10 ozs pasta of choice
Parmesan cheese

Beat or blend cottage cheese and cream cheese until smooth. Sauté onion and mushrooms in butter; stir in wine and seasonings. Stir in cheese mixture with milk and heat through. Chop spinach and drain well; add to sauce and heat. Serve over hot cooked pasta and sprinkle with Parmesan cheese, if desired.

119 SPINACH LASAGNA PINWHEELS

Neat green and white individual servings

12 lasagna noodles, cooked and drained
1 lb fresh spinach, or 2, 10 oz pkgs frozen spinach, cooked and drained
2 lbs Ricotta cheese
2 eggs
1 T chopped fresh parsley, or 1 t dried parsley
salt, pepper and garlic salt to taste
1 lb Monterey Jack cheese, shredded
1 C grated Parmesan cheese
2 T melted margarine

Chop spinach and combine with Ricotta cheese, eggs and seasonings. Spoon mixture in a thin layer on the length of each noodle. Roll up and place finished rolls in a greased 13X9 pan. Sprinkle with both Monterey Jack and Parmesan cheeses. Drizzle top with melted butter. Bake at 350° for 30-45 minutes. Serves 12.

120 SPINACH PUDDING OR PIE

1 lb cooked fresh spinach, or 2, 10 oz pkgs frozen spinach
2 C cottage cheese, or Ricotta cheese
1 t salt
1/3 C Parmesan cheese
2 eggs

Mix all ingredients and bake in greased casserole or a unbaked pieshell at 350° for 30 minutes.

121 GREEN RICE

4 C rice
1 C cooked spinach
1 C shredded Cheddar cheese
1/2 C Parmesan cheese
1/2 C sliced green onions

Mix all ingredients and spread in a buttered casserole. Bake at 350° until heated through and bubbly.

is for Squash

What do you need to know about squash? Two of the softshelled summer squash are *zucchini*, and yellow squash shaped like zucchini, usually just called *"summer squash."* These are best used when small, and are sliced and eaten without peeling, either raw or cooked. Hard shelled or "winter squash" grow in all shapes and colors. They are peeled, either before or after cooking, and the meat varies from delicate yellow to deep gold. When a recipe calls for squash, it usually means winter squash. The basic differences in the varieties is taste and degree of stringiness and moisture. *Acorn*, dark green with deep ridges is often just cut in half, seeds removed and centers are filled with goodies. They are baked and eaten from the shell. Don't confuse butternut and buttercup. *Buttercup* looks like a small drum with a little crown on top. *Butternut* most resembles a dull yellow bowling pin with a thick neck. The neck is solid flesh. *Hubbard* squash are the giant green and orange fellas and have sweet orange flesh. All winter squash can be just tossed in the oven and baked in the shell. When tender, cut and remove seeds and skin. Then the meat can be mashed or whipped with butter and seasonings. The microwave is a wonderful way to cook whole squash. Just prick the skin and microwave until tender. If you'd rather, just cut squash open, remove seeds, peel and cook chunks as you would potatoes. ***Season squash with maple syrup, butter, brown sugar, pecans, allspice, cinnamon, cloves, ginger, and, nutmeg.***

122 BUTTERNUT SQUASH SOUP

Squash keeps for a long time in a cool place. Make this on fall days after the summer rush is over

1 medium butternut squash
3 tart apples
1 medium onion
1/2 t nutmeg
salt and pepper to taste

2 C rich broth
2 C water
1/2 C evaporated milk
fresh parsley for garnish

Peel squash, remove seeds and cut in chunks. Peel and dice apple and onion. Combine prepared squash, apples and onion and simmer in broth with seasonings until tender, about 45 minutes. Purée mixture in blender or food processor and return to pan; add milk and adjust seasonings to taste. Serve hot with a sprinkle of parsley. Serves 6.

123 SQUASH DRESSING

Leftover cornbread and squash for dinner tonight

3 C corn bread crumbs
1 t sage
1/4 C margarine
1 can cream of mushroom soup

2 1/2 C cooked squash
1 C sour cream
1 small onion, chopped
2 carrots, shredded

Sauté onions in margarine; add rest of ingredients and pour into a buttered baking dish. Bake at 350° for 40 minutes.

124 STUFFED ACORNS

2 acorn squash
4 T butter or margarine
4 t lemon juice

nutmeg
4-8 T brown sugar*
4 T chopped pecans

Cut squash in half lengthwise and scoop out seeds. Sprinkle each half with 1 teaspoon lemon juice and a little nutmeg. Add 1 tablespoon butter, 1-2 tablespoons brown sugar and 1 tablespoon pecans to each cavity. Bake uncovered at 350° for 35-40 minutes or until tender. Serves 4.
Can substitute maple syrup or pancake syrup.

is for Sweet Potatoes

Sweet potatoes are one of the most nutritious vegetables of them all. Cook them in their skins to preserve vitamins and flavor. Call them yams if you like, but they are not yams, and don't store them in the refrigerator. Candied sweet potatoes are the classic holiday dish, but try them all year round. Baked, they are delicious skin and all, or stuff them with butter, seasonings and toasted almonds. Combine them with carrots and apples in casseroles; slice cold boiled sweet potatoes and sauté in butter, or make a southern sweet potato pie.

125 PINEAPPLE STUFFED SWEET POTATOES

A sweet main dish without lots of extra sugar

3 large sweet potatoes
1 T butter
1/2 t salt
1 T cream

1/2 C drained crushed pineapple
24 miniature marshmallows
2 T hot pineapple juice

Scrub and bake potatoes at 450° until done. Split lengthwise and scoop out centers, leaving a shell. Mash potato with butter, salt, cream and pineapple; refill potato skins and top with marshmallows. Place in a pan, bake at 325° for 20 minutes, basting with hot pineapple juice. Serves 6.

126 CRISPY SWEET POTATO BAKE

3 C mashed sweet potato
3 T butter
1/2 C sugar
2 eggs, beaten
1/2 C milk
1/2 t each salt and cinnamon

Topping:
1/2 C brown sugar
2 1/2 T flour
2 T butter
1/2 C chopped pecans

Combine all ingredients except topping and beat with a mixer until fluffy. Pour into a buttered casserole. Mix topping ingredients until crumbly; sprinkle over sweet potatoes and bake at 375° for 25 minutes.

127 SWEET POTATO PIE

6-8 medium sweet potatoes
2 t vanilla
8 T brown sugar
6 T butter
1 t cinnamon

1/2 t each salt and nutmeg
3 eggs, separated
3 C milk
1, 9-10 inch unbaked pie shell

Cook, peel and mash potatoes; add vanilla, sugar, butter and spices. Beat egg yolks until light and add milk. Add potato mixture and mix until light. Beat egg whites stiff and fold into potato mixture. Pour into pie shell and bake at 350° for 1 hour.

is for Tomato

How could we cook without this fruit also called the "love apple?" We use it as a main dish, both hot and cold, cooked in other things, a base for soup, and, consider it a necessity for sandwiches and salads. Tomatoes are easily peeled after a quick dip in boiling water. It is no wonder that tomatoes grow in abundance in a million gardens. ***Seasonings good with tomatoes are basil, bay leaves, celery seed, oregano, cilantro, sage, and thyme.***

128 BROILED RIPE TOMATOES

4 large ripe tomatoes
salt and pepper to taste
Dijon mustard

6 t melted margarine
1/2 C seasoned bread crumbs
1/2 C Parmesan cheese

Preheat broiler. Cut tomatoes in half; spread with mustard and sprinkle with salt and pepper. Combine butter, crumbs and cheese; spoon on tomato halves. Broil for 8-10 minutes.

129 FRIED GREEN TOMATOES

From the movie of the same name

Cut tomatoes in 1/2 inch slices. Dip in flour seasoned with salt and pepper. Fry slowly in a small amount of hot fat until browned on both sides.

130 CHEESY TOMATO SOUP

Crock pot soup for a crowd

10 medium ripe tomatoes
2 T melted butter
1 medium onion, chopped
1 clove garlic, minced
2 T flour

2 t sugar
8 C bouillon
2 T parsley
1/2 t each thyme,
   basil and rosemary
1, 8 oz pkg cream cheese

Remove stems, cut tomatoes in quarters and bake in a covered dish at 325° for 20 minutes. Remove skins and let cool. Sauté onion and garlic in butter until softened; add flour and sugar and mix well. Stir bouillon into mixture and add spices. In small portions, blend the bouillon mixture and tomatoes until all are blended, adding cheese to last batch. Simmer soup in a slow cooker for 2 hours.

131 GARDEN VEGETABLE SOUP

A bowl full of vitamins

3 qts tomatoes	1 C chopped onion
1 qt water	1 C sliced celery
2 T parsley flakes	2 C sliced carrot
1 bay leaf	2 C cubed turnip
1 t thyme	3 C cubed potato
1 t ground cloves	1/2 C barley
salt and pepper to taste	3 C shredded cabbage

Put all ingredients except barley and cabbage in a soup pot and bring to a boil. Simmer for 15-20 minutes. Add barley and cook until barley is done, about 45 minutes. Adjust seasoning and remove bay leaf. Place 3-4 tablespoons of finely shredded raw cabbage in each bowl and ladle hot soup over cabbage. (The hot soup wilts the cabbage.) Serve with hot corn bread. Serves 8-10.

132   RAW MEXICAN SALSA

Make your own and enjoy it north of the border

2 medium, unpeeled tomatoes
1 medium sweet onion
1 clove garlic, minced or pressed
2-4 fresh jalapeno peppers
1 T snipped fresh cilantro
1 T lemon juice
1 1/2 t oil
1/2 t oregano

Dice vegetables finely, using peppers to desired hotness. *If you like really hot salsa, use seeds and membrane of peppers and wear plastic gloves to dice them.* Add remaining ingredients (the cilantro is a must) and chill for 1 hour. Serve with tortilla chips, tacos or on scrambled eggs.

133   GAZPACHO

Delicious cold soup for a hot day

1 clove garlic
1 T sugar
1 1/2 t salt
5 C tomato juice
2 T vegetable oil
2 T lemon juice
1 t Worcestershire sauce
3 tomatoes finely chopped
1 cucumber, peeled and diced
1 green pepper, finely diced
1 C shredded carrot
1 C thinly sliced celery
1/4 C thinly sliced onion

Chop, then mash garlic; blend or beat with sugar, salt, juices, oil and Worcestershire sauce. Stir in prepared vegetables and chill for several hours. This keeps for 3-4 days in refrigerator. Serves 10.

134 SPINACH STUFFED TOMATOES

Stuff these pretties ahead for a dinner party

6 medium tomatoes
salt
6 T butter
1 medium onion
6 T flour
1 1/2 C milk

salt and pepper to taste
1 t Worcestershire sauce
2 t lemon juice
2, 10 oz pkgs frozen
    chopped spinach

Wash tomatoes and cut core from tops; carefully hollow out inside with a teaspoon, leaving a shell. Sprinkle insides of shells with salt and turn upside down on paper towels to drain. Sauté onions in butter until transparent; remove from heat and blend in flour, then milk, stirring well to prevent lumps. Cook until bubbly, adding salt, pepper, Worcestershire sauce and lemon juice. Cook spinach; drain and squeeze out as much moisture as possible. Add spinach to white sauce and mix well. Spoon mixture into tomato shells and arrange them close together in a shallow pan. Pour 1/2 C water in bottom of pan. Bake at 350° for 30 minutes. Remove to serving dish with a slotted spoon. Serves 6.

is for Turnips

Turnips are pretty in centerpieces with their purple tops and white bottoms. This plentiful source of vitamin C is good sliced and eaten raw, good in salads and is especially good in soups and stews. Don't overcook turnips, cook just until tender. Serve them creamed with peas and mashed with carrots. **Season turnips with onion salt, lemon juice, paprika and pepper.**

135 MASHED TURNIPS AND CARROTS

4-5 medium turnips
6 large carrots
2 T sugar
salt to taste
1 medium onion
3 T butter

Peel and halve the turnips and carrots; cook in boiling water until tender. Mash while hot and add sugar and salt to taste. Sauté onion in butter and add to turnips and carrots. Serves 6-8.

136 BUTTERED TURNIPS

6 medium turnips
2 T butter
1 T lemon juice
1 T dried parsley
1 t paprika

Peel, quarter and cook turnips until just tender; drain well. Melt butter, add lemon juice and parsley. Toss with hot turnips. Place in a serving dish and sprinkle with paprika.

is for Zucchini

Yes, it is one of the summer squash, but it makes such a nice "Z" for an alphabetical book. This prolific fellow will take over your garden and start for the neighbor's, so be careful how many you plant. Try and pick when they are 4-9 inches long, but you must watch closely, they grow like lightening!

137 QUICK ZUCCHINI PICKLES

1/2 C cider vinegar
1/2 C water
1/3 C sugar
3 T diced green onion
1/2 t salt
1 clove garlic, minced
1/2 t celery seed
3 medium zucchini, sliced and placed in a glass jar or container.

Heat other ingredients to a boil and pour over zucchini. Let stand 3-4 days before eating.

138 ZUCCHINI RELISH

10 C ground zucchini
4 C ground onions
5 T salt
2 1/4 C vinegar
4 C sugar
1 T ground nutmeg

1 T turmeric
1 T celery seeds
1 T black pepper
1 T dry mustard
2 green peppers
2 red peppers

Stir salt into ground vegetables and let stand overnight. Drain. Rinse squash in cold water; drain mixture in cheesecloth. Combine squash mixture and remaining ingredients in a large Dutch oven and heat to boiling. Simmer for 30 minutes. Pour into sterilized jars and seal. Makes 7 pints.

139 GOOD ZUCCHINI STUFF I

Garden to table and delicious

3-4 medium unpeeled zuchini, cubed
1 medium onion, diced
1 green pepper, diced
2-3 tomatoes, diced
salt, pepper and basil
1/2 C shredded cheddar cheese

Put all ingredients except cheese in a saucepan and bring to a boil. (Do not add water.) Cook until zucchini is transparent. Stir in cheese and serve. Serves 5.

140 GOOD ZUCCHINI STUFF II

Habit forming!

1 C medium Cheddar cheese, cubed
1 C cooked brown rice
2 lbs thinly sliced zucchini
1/2 C slices green onion
1 t salt
1/2 t garlic powder
1 t dried sweet basil
2 beaten eggs

Mix all ingredients together lightly. Place in oiled casserole dish. Bake at 350° for 1 hour. Serves 6.

141 GARDEN GOULASH

2 C diced zucchini
1/2 C chopped onion
1/2 t basil leaves
2 T butter
1 can Cheddar cheese soup

3 C elbow macaroni
2 C sharp Cheddar cheese
2 C stewed tomatoes
1/2 t prepared mustard

Cook zucchini and onion with basil in butter until tender. Add remaining ingredients. Heat until cheese melts; stir often. Serves 5-8.

142 ZUCCHINI AND CHEESE

2 or 3 small zucchini, shredded
1 C shredded Monterey Jack cheese
2 eggs

1/4 C chopped parsley
salt, pepper and butter

Sprinkle some salt lightly over squash in a flat dish and let stand for 1 hour. Squeeze out as much liquid as possible using the back of a large spoon. Add parsley, cheese, eggs, and season to taste, mixing well. Pour into a buttered 8X8 baking dish and dot with butter. Bake at 350° for about 40 minutes until squash is tender and top browned.

143 ZUCCHINI LASAGNA

3-4 medium zucchini
1, 30 oz jar spaghetti sauce
1, 6 oz can tomato paste
1, 16 oz pkg lasagna noodles
2 eggs

2 C Ricotta cheese
1/2 C Parmesan cheese
2 T parsley flakes or fresh parsley
1 lb shredded Mozzarella cheese

Cut zucchini (peeled or unpeeled) lengthwise in 1/4 inch slices; cook in a large sauce pan for about 5 minutes and drain well. Cook noodles and drain. Combine eggs, cheeses and parsley. Combine spaghetti sauce and tomato paste. Grease a 9X13 pan and spread some sauce in bottom of pan; make layers of 1/3 of noodles, 1/3 of cheese mixture, 1/2 of zucchini slices, and 1/3 of sauce, ending with noodles sauce and cheese. Cover with foil and Bake at 350° for 30 minutes.

144 ZUCCHINI MUSHROOM BAKE

For lunch or a party appetizer

3 T olive oil
2 C thinly sliced zucchini
1 C sliced fresh mushrooms
2/3 C sliced green onions
1/3 C minced fresh parsley

2 cloves garlic, mashed
7-8 beaten eggs
3/4 C Parmesan cheese
1/2 t each basil and salt
black pepper to taste

Sauté zucchini, mushrooms, onion, parsley and garlic in oil. Combine with eggs and remaining ingredients. Pour into a greased 9X9 pan. Bake at 350° for 20-25 minutes. Serve hot or cold.

145 ZUCCHINI PIZZA

2 C thinly sliced zucchini
1 medium onion, chopped
1/2 C chopped fresh parsley
  or 3 T dried parsley
1-2 cloves garlic, pressed
1 C baking mix

1/2 C salad oil
1 t oregano
salt to taste
1/2 C Parmesan cheese
4 eggs, slightly beaten
2 t paprika

Put all ingredients except paprika in a large bowl and stir to blend. Pour into a greased 9X13 pan and bake at 350° for 35 minutes. Cool and cut into squares. Good hot or cold.

146 ZUCCHINI BREAD

1 C white flour
1 1/2 t baking powder
1/2 t soda
1/2 t salt
1 t cinnamon
1 C whole wheat flour
2 eggs

2/3 C oil
1/4 C honey
1/2 t lemon extract
1 1/2 C shredded zucchini
1/2 C chopped nuts
1/4 C raisins
1 t sesame seeds

Mix together dry ingredients. Beat eggs, oil, honey and lemon extract until smooth. Stir in zucchini; add flour mixture and stir well but do not beat. Stir in nuts and raisins. Pour into a greased loaf pan and bake at 325° for 1 hour or until loaf tests done.

147 FROSTED ZUCCHINI BARS

3/4 C margarine
1/2 C brown sugar
1/2 C white sugar
2 eggs
1 t vanilla

1 3/4 C flour
1 1/2 t baking powder
2 C shredded zucchini
1 C coconut*
3/4 C chopped nuts

Cream margarine and sugar until blended; add eggs and vanilla, beating until smooth. Sift flour and baking powder and stir into creamed mixture. Stir in remaining ingredients. Spread into a greased jelly roll pan and bake at 350° for 35-40 minutes. Frost while warm.
1/2 C chopped dates, or other dried fruit may be substituted for coconut.
Frosting: 1 C powdered sugar, 2 1/2 T milk, 1 1/2 T melted margarine, 1 t vanilla, 1/2 t cinnamon.

The Big Fat Red Juicy Apple Cook Book
Tasty Taters
Say Cheese
Catch of the Day - Fish & Seafood Cook Book
The Very Berry Cook Book
Merry Cookie!
BBQ Cooking
Daily Bread
Just Peachy
Salad Chef
The Garden Cart Vegetarian Cook Book
The Cookie Book